Special Tax Commission

Report of the special tax commission of Maine; appointed under resolve of the legislature,

Approved March 8th, 1889

Special Tax Commission

Report of the special tax commission of Maine; appointed under resolve of the legislature, *Approved March 8th, 1889*

ISBN/EAN: 9783744722803

Printed in Europe, USA, Canada, Australia, Japan

Cover: Foto ©Suzi / pixelio.de

More available books at **www.hansebooks.com**

REPORT

OF THE

Special Tax Commission of Maine,

APPOINTED UNDER

RESOLVE OF THE LEGISLATURE,

Approved March 8th, 1889.

———— —•· ·———

AUGUSTA:
BURLEIGH & FLYNT, PRINTERS TO THE STATE.
1890.

RESOLVE.

To provide a Commission to inquire into the system of taxation of other states and this state and report to the Governor and Council.

Resolved, That the governor be and hereby is, by and with the consent of the council authorized and empowered to appoint a commission consisting of three persons whose duty it shall be to inquire into the system adopted by other states to raise revenue for state, county and municipal expenses, and to provide for a more equal, just and equitable system of taxation, of all kinds of property in this state, for the purposes of said state, county and municipal expenses, that shall be better adapted to the wants of this state and reduce the rate of taxation of the people; and to provide for a better, and more effectual system of assessment and collection of taxes, in this state; said commissioners to be paid from any money in the state treasury not otherwise appropriated, such a sum for their services as shall be allowed by the governor and council and for necessary clerk hire and incidental expenses and to report to the governor and council on or before the first day of October in the year of our Lord eighteen hundred and ninety; and that the governor shall cause their report to be printed and distributed at the state's expense, three copies of which shall be sent by mail or otherwise to each member of the present legislature to their proper residence; and one thousand copies of said report shall be provided for the use of the next legislature of this state.

Approved March 8, 1889.

REPORT.

To the Honorable Edwin C. Burleigh, Governor of the State of Maine:

The Commissioners appointed by your Excellency under the foregoing resolve of the Sixty-Fourth Legislature organized on the nineteenth of November, 1889, and at once began an examination of the general subject of taxation, within the scope of the resolve, which is sufficiently broad to allow all necessary research for improved methods. Our first endeavor was to determine what were the defects of our present system which afford just cause for complaint, and which, in the judgment of the legislature, make the inquiry necessary. The Commission selected A. M. Goddard, Esq., of Augusta, as its clerk whose services have been efficient and valuable.

To acquire the desired information, we began to hold meetings of the Commission at the State House in Augusta, in December, 1889, for the purpose of hearing parties desiring to be heard and for discussion. We invited discussions through the press of the State by notice in the leading newspapers of the several sections and sought, by correspondence and interviews with persons whom we thought to have had experience in matters of taxation and by circulars of interrogatories to boards of assessors, to inform ourselves in relation to the particular provisions of our present statute which are defective or inadequate and as to its deficiencies. After an extended investigation of this kind, we began an examination into the systems of taxation in vogue elsewhere in this country, and to do this systematically and in such way as to gain the most information in the time allotted us, we proceeded to collate and arrange in order an epitome of so much of the tax laws now in force in the several states as are materially different from those of Maine. We did not deem it essential to extend this inquiry into every one of the states, yet it was necessary to make the examination widely comprehensive, and the laws of every state which included any features which we believed it desirable to incorporate into the system of this State, we have examined with care. Having so examined the laws of the several states sufficiently to acquire a general knowledge, at least, of the several revenue systems, we visited several states, whose systems contain features radically different from ours, for the purpose of getting definite information as to the practical workings of such systems. For this purpose, New Hampshire, Vermont, Massachusetts, Connecticut, Rhode Island and New York were visited, which states represent very well the more pronounced differences of method in raising revenues, as employed in the United States, both for state and local purposes. We have also studied with an anxious desire to learn of some method yet untried in this State, which contains the promise of practical efficiency, the theories of several prominent economists and writers upon social science.

SYSTEMS OF TAXATION.

The disposition to conceal property from the assessor has always prevailed. Even in the primitive days of New England, when the forms of taxable property were few, extraordinary methods had to be resorted to to bring all the taxable property under assessment. Perhaps as curious a tax law as any ,was that of Rhode Island passed in 1673, as follows :

"If the Assembly judge any have undervalued their estate, each shall be required to give in to the Treasurer a true form of an Inventory of all their Estates and Strength in particular, and give in writing what proportion of Estate and Strength in particular he *guesseth ten of his neighbors, naming them in particular, hath in Estate and Strength to his Estate and Strength.*"

If property should now be assessed at a valuation set by ones' neighbors, there would be plenty of revenue.

The present system of taxation in this State is substantially that borrowed from Massachusetts at the time of the separation, and is the result of an attempt to enforce the principles of the first tax law adopted by the General Court of Massachusetts Bay, whereby it was enacted :

"That every Inhabitant shall Contribute to all Charges both in Church and Common-wealth, whereof he doth or may receive benefit. And every such Inhabitant who shall not Contribute proportionably to his ability to all common Charges, both Civil and Ecclesiastical, shall be compelled thereunto, by Assessment and Distress, to be levied by the Constable or other officer of the Town."

The Commonwealth of Massachusetts embodied this rule of taxation in the Constitution of 1780 in granting the General Court "power and authority to impose and levy proportional and reasonable rates, assessments, and taxes upon all the inhabitants of and persons resident, and estates lying in said Common-wealth."

It was expressed in the original Constitution of Maine, Art. IX, Sec. 8, as follows : "All taxes upon real estate, assessed by authority of this State, shall be apportioned and assessed equally, according to the just value thereof." Although personal estate was not mentioned in the Constitution as subject to equality of taxation, the first tax laws enacted by the legislature after its adoption included as taxable "all estates real and personal" not by law exempted ; and by the seventeenth amendment of the Constitution, adopted in 1875, Sec. 8 of Art. IX, equality of apportionment and assessment was made to cover personal as well as real estate. This principle of our system and many of its details remain as in 1821. They have been in vogue during the entire life of the State and were substantially the laws of our ancestors under Massachusetts from the beginning. The only alterations have been the engrafting upon the system, from time to time, of amendments which were devised to meet the altered conditions of business and business methods, mainly from the great and multiplying interests of corporations and in the attempt to bring into the assessment lists the rapidly increasing, intangible wealth of recent years.

While we have not been unmindful of the various latter-day theories of political economists relating to this complicated subject, and confess to having been compelled to acknowledge the logical soundness of many views advanced, which are at variance with the conclusions at which we have arrived, yet, after such deliberation and study of the perplexing facts involved as we have been able to give them, we have decided that it were better to err upon the side of conservatism, in a matter so far reaching and important as this, and bear some of the ills of a time-honored system, "than fly to others that we know not of." "A system," says an able writer upon the Inequalities of Taxation in Massachusetts, "which has been thus developed by the experience of an intelligent and practical people during so long a period, and to which all social and business interests have become adapted, cannot safely be essentially changed except by a gradual and experimental process.'

We have also believed it inexpedient to recommend any changes of the law which cannot be made without changes in the Constitution. Yet we have not been so conservative as to hesitate to recommend a radical change in several respects, where an antiquated method, unsatisfactory in results, could be readily altered to a method which in many states has been found to yield excellent results, and involving no constitutional objections. In other words, our veneration for the old has not prevented our acceptance and recommendation of several important changes in our system, where the practical experience of other states has shown such change to be safe and salutary. The principal changes of this kind which we have embodied in the proposed act herewith submitted, are the provisions for a permanent board of State Assessors, and a new method of State valuation and equalization. Our present system lacks a head—a central, controlling supervision of the important details so necessary to render any financial system, and much more a system so far reaching and vital as that of raising revenue, efficient. This we have tried to remedy in the bill herewith.

The other changes, which are quite numerous, are in the nature of amendments and additions to the present system, so as to include new sources of revenue, and especially by making the listing of property more peremptory and effective.

The tendency of the theories of many able writers upon the tax problem is towards the single tax—a tax on land values. Indeed, that is the system which most European countries have now adopted, relieving all money, evidences of debt, and in some instances all personal property, from any taxation whatever. In view of the prominence this theory is assuming in this country at present, we have felt it our duty to examine it, although mindful of the instructions of the resolve under which we were acting, "to provide for a more equal, just and equitable system of taxation *of all kinds* of property." It is by no means new. Judge Cooley, whose legal works are standard in the courts of the country, writing in 1876, after enumerating several principal objections to the assessment of personal property—that it must necessarily be inquisitorial in its operation; that it destroys privacy in business and family concerns; induces false swearing; leads to fraud; often discriminates unjustly between residents and non-residents; leads to double taxation, and requires a larger force and more frequent assessments than would otherwise be necessary—says: "These are objections which every one feels and appreciates; others, which are more obscure, need not be mentioned. A tax on land is not open to these objections. Whenever the law seeks to tax land and personalty with equality, the land pays much the greater portion of the tax, because this can all be reached and all be taxed; no inquisitorial proceedings are required to discover it, and no frauds or evasions can conceal it from view. These and other reasons have led some political economists to advocate the omission of personalty from the customary taxation by value, and the raising of the ordinary state revenue by tax laid exclusively on land and a few other objects which, like land, are open to constant public observation and inspection, and in respect to which neither would harsh sifting processes be required, nor evasions be practicable, nor frauds invited. Such a tax, it is claimed, while nominally falling upon a few, would in fact be diffused through the whole community, and collected from all by being added to the price of what is produced and distributed by the classes taxed, just as we have found that a tax upon any common article of consumption is paid in the end by the consumer, and is no more burdensome to the dealer who nominally pays it than it is to any other member of the community of consumers." *Cooley on Taxation, Ch. I, Page* 29. While this distinguished author does not directly indorse the single tax theory, he makes it appear very alluring. The above very fairly states the substance of the Henry George theory, excepting that the distinguished Single Tax apostle denies that the tax on land values is shifted to the consumer.

President Ely of Johns Hopkins University, a prominent author of social science works, in a supplemental report as one of the Tax Commissioners of Maryland, while not approving the single tax theory, yet advocates with great force a system which should "assess to the last dollar of its true value all real estate held for speculative purposes," and would have land bear by far the greater share of the public burden and would specially exempt altogether from assessment mortgages, promissory notes, book accounts, simple contract debts and other private securities, and he lays it down as one of the fundamental principles of his system that as few things as possible should be taxed and that "in the selection of objects for taxation great care should be taken to reduce interference with business and professional pursuits to a minimum."

An intelligent advocate of the single tax system residing in Knox county, in a letter to the Commissioners bespeaking for the system the attention of the Commission, gives an outline of it as follows :

"Taxes on the products of labor tend to restrict production. To one who has given that study which you have done to economic questions, it is unnecessary to argue this point. You will, I am sure, accept it as established at the start. Therefore, it is urged, no taxes should be imposed on improvements or commodities, if the necessary revenues can be obtained without resorting to that source.

"A tax on land values does not restrict production or lessen the reward of the users of land as such. On the contrary, by making it unprofitable to hold land out of use, it always operates to open natural opportunities for labor and capital, and so stimulates production. Therefore, all taxes should be levied on land values, and none on the fruits of industry till the full rental value of land is taken for the purpose and proves insufficient in amount. We believe that it would be amply sufficient.

"Every man is entitled to the full results of his own labor or enterprise in producing wealth; but that value which attaches to land by reason of the increased competition for the privilege of using it, and which is due to the growth of population and public improvements, justly belongs to the whole community. Therefore, the public should take by taxation the full rental value of land, at least to the extent of the revenue needed for all purposes of government and the cost of all public improvements.

"Government being supported by the ground rent, now going as 'unearned increment' to individuals, and industry being relieved from taxation, land speculation would cease and natural opportunities be opened to labor. Workmen unable to get the wages they should, would be able to employ themselves and receive the full product of their labor, and capital would enjoy the same advantage, being relieved of the landlords' tribute. There could then be no lack of employment, and wages would rise to their natural level, the full earnings of labor. The labor problem is, how shall all men willing to work always find opportunities to do so and thus produce the wealth that they need? The single tax would, it is claimed, solve that problem.

"This argument is presented completely and most ably in the great work of Henry George, 'Progress and Poverty,' and I trust you will not permit the Commission to make a report to legislature without giving a fair and unprejudiced consideration to the fact adduced and the reasoning contained in that book."

A prominent lawyer in Penobscot, in an able paper read before an agricultural society two years since, condemned our laws taxing personal property, and recommended the single land tax as not open to objection, but concluded by stating the very obvious fact, that such a tax "could not be practicable, however, unless adopted by all the states." The era of inter-state uniformity of tax laws is yet exceedingly remote, and so is the millennium. Another great hindrance to the adoption of "a land-tax-only" system is the wide disparity of condition between the great business centres and the village and rural districts. The farmer or village resident whose property "all lies out of doors" cannot be induced to look with favor upon a system which would tax his farm to its utmost value, while the money, bank stock, piano, fine horses and carriages and stock in trade of his wealthier neighbor were passed over by the assessor. We cannot believe that the time has yet arrived when such a system is adapted to a state like ours, and we are very positive that Maine would refuse to lead in a system entirely untried by any state in the Union.

In spite of the theories of the many brilliant writers on taxation for half a century, and notwithstanding the obnoxious features of a general property tax have long been held up to the people as the embodiment of all that is iniquitous in morals and destructive of business prosperity, no state has yet turned from the evil of its ways in enforcing its revenues, in part at least, from personal property. Indeed this method is becoming yearly more fixed and general. It has come to be recognized as the American system as distinguished from the systems of other governments where the objects of taxation are fewer and where property is rated at its income value rather than at its selling value. We believe the people of this State do not desire to abandon the general tax system. In view of that fact, our object and effort has been to adapt the laws to the system. If a large portion of the revenues must necessarily continue to be raised from a general property tax, the laws must be made to reach the property. We have no sympathy with the idea that because some men will defraud the revenue; because they will conceal property, commit perjury and resort to all conceivable trickery to prevent taxation, therefore the whole classes of property which they would thus hide from the assessor should be exempted by law.

The substance of the complaint in Maine is that personal property is not reached for taxation; that those who have most of it escape their just portion of the burdens of the government; that in consequence, real estate and tangible personal property, such as the farmer and the village real property owners possess, bear an undue burden. If this complaint is just, then the remedy is evident, make a law which shall bring the personal property to the attention of the assessors and oblige them to apportion and assess it, as the Constitution requires, "equally, according to the just value thereof." This complaint is unquestionably well founded. It is a notorious fact proven by all revenue statistics, that not only in this State, but in all the states, the percentage of revenue from personal property, relative to real, is growing less. Indeed, it seems well understood and believed that nothing more is necessary to be done in the way of statute remedies than to provide some means to make personal bear its equal burden with real property. In that direction all efforts for improvement in the laws of the several states are tending. It is in that line that we have wrought out the results we have reached.

If the tax valuations of personal property of the whole country were to be consulted for the purpose of ascertaining its financial condition, it would be found to be hopelessly speeding towards bankruptcy. From 1870 to 1880, according to the census returns, the assessed valuation of the personal property of all the states decreased from $5,111,554,000, to $3,866,227,-000, while the assessed value of real estate increased more than five billions. It was seen by these figures that new methods must be resorted to by state legislatures to compel personal property, especially intangible kinds, to bear a more equal share of the burdens. The tax problem at once became a more important one than ever before. State pride was touched. Tax commissions were appointed in many states and vigorous efforts made to prevent such a fallacious representation of their resources. More rigorous laws were enacted to compel disclosures of property and to hold assessors to their duties. Among the states which have adopted radical changes in their assessment laws since 1880 are New York, Massachusetts, Maryland, Connecticut, Vermont, Ohio, Virginia, Wisconsin, Michigan, North Carolina and Pennsylvania.

THE REMEDY.

It is evident, then, that whatever remedies law can supply, under our system of general property taxation, must be in the direction of *equality* of taxation. That all taxable property is not equally assessed under our present laws, and that land and houses and cattle, visible and tangible property, are bearing an unequal share of the public burdens ; and that farmers especially, as a prominent stock raiser concisely puts it, are "drawing at the short end of the yoke," all concede. That this complaint of the escape of much personal estate from taxation, and the demand for a remedy, has not been a mere partisan cry, but a well founded desire for a much needed reform, is apparent from the following extracts from the recommendations of our governors, of both parties, during the last sixteen years, in their messages to the legislature :

[*Gov. Dingley*, 1874.]

"I most earnestly urge that you should consider whether it is not advisable to devise some method other than direct taxation to secure a part of the revenue required for State expenditures ; so that the rate of taxation may be still further reduced. Pennsylvania finds no difficulty in securing sufficient receipts from indirect taxation to support the state government. A large share of the state expenditures of

Massachusetts is met by the proceeds of a state tax upon the valuation of the corporate stock of railroad and other corporations over and above municipal taxation for real estate and machinery; and upon the business of fire and life insurance companies. Without indicating more in detail what sources of revenue may be made available to this State, I desire to call your attention to the subject, and to suggest a careful inquiry and investigation, with a view of devising methods of lifting some portion of the burden of taxation from real estate. Such a policy would give needed encouragement to our agricultural interests, and promote the development of the resources of the State."

[*Gov. Dingley*, 1875.]

"Without such a radical reformation as will lead all men to be honest and truthful in rendering statements of their property, it is of course impossible to devise any system of taxation which will be absolutely equal; as capital which is represented by stocks, bonds, loans and currency, can not be reached by the assessor as readily as that invested in farms, houses, stores, mills, work-shops, ships and other visible property. At the same time, this liability to inequality should be corrected so far as it is possible. So far as capital is invested, directly or indirectly, in banking, railroad, telegraph, express and insurance business, it may and should be reached. The last legislature inaugurated steps in the right direction with reference to a part of these interests. I earnestly hope that you will continue to press forward measures looking to such a system of taxation as will tend to equalize the public burdens."

[*Gov. Garcelon*, 1879.]

"The average rate of taxation upon real estate and farm property for a series of years has not been less than one and one-half per cent. During the same time a very large proportion of the accumulated capital of the State has been virtually exempt from all assessments. Probably more than one hundred millions of the accumulated wealth of this State is invested in mortgages, railroad, municipal, county and State bonds, or deposited in savings banks, and it would seem but an act of justice to enact such laws, if practicable, as will compel the holders of such property to bear their just proportion of the public burdens."

[*Gov. Davis*, 1880.]

"The burdens of taxation press heavily upon the people. Every species of property, whether owned by individuals or corporations, should bear its part of the public burden. If there is any property in the State not yet reached by the tax gatherer, or which does not bear its proportionate part, it is your province to ascertain that fact, and make such changes in the laws as may be necessary."

[*Gov. Plaisted*, 1881.]

"Too large a proportion of the public burden falls upon real estate. This is especially true of all farm property. The property of the farmer is all visible and exposed to assessment.

    *   *   •   *   *   *   *

It is not in the economical expenditure of the public revenue, so much as in seeking new sources of revenues and in equalizing the burdens of taxation, that you will be able to compass such reforms and such relief as will gladden the hearts and cheer the hopes of our people. The public burdens are unequally borne. When all the property in the State is reached and taxed as real estate and all property of farmers "according to the just value thereof," the rate of taxation will be reduced one-half. Then will taxation fall lightly and be borne cheerfully, because it will fall equally upon all. True it is, that absolute equality in taxation can never be attained. A disproportionate share of the public burdens will always be thrown on certain kinds of property because they are visible and tangible. The best system to be sought is that which, in its practical operation, approximates nearest to equality."

[*Gov. Robie*, 1883.]

"The legislature of 1874 inaugurated a new system of taxation, seeking to equalize it by removing a part of the burden from the productive industries of the State and transferring it to capital invested in railroad, telegraph, express and insurance companies, savings banks, and like corporations and business. By repeated changes of law, a system of taxation has been legalized and sustained by the constitutional authorities of the State, which has brought a new revenue into our treasury, and thereby lightened the burden on visible property.

"The State of Vermont has already provided, by a tax on these several interests, a sum sufficient for all the State expenditures without assessing a single dollar on the several towns and cities.

"I would suggest that the legislature investigate the present system of taxation, as far as practicable, that measures may be devised to provide that all kinds of property and interests be reached, so that, in a just way, public burdens may be equalized."

[*Gov. Bodwell,* 1887.]

"It may be stated as a maxim that there is no expenditure for which the citizen gets so much in return as for the amount he devotes to paying taxes, and yet there is no subject upon which people are more justly sensitive than that the taxes be equal. If all communities, and all the citizens of each community, paid in equal and proper proportion, there would be no complaint among the people. The grievance arises, in large part, from the inequality of taxation, and the inequality arises, in large part, from the errors in valuation—errors in many cases innocently made, no doubt, but still working hardship in many ways."

[*Gov. Burleigh,* 1889.]

"Our own State valuation finds too large a proportion of our property in the farms of the State and makes the farmers pay an undue share of the general taxes. On the other hand the valuation of the United States Census takes cognizance of the less tangible but more profitable investments which escape their fair share of the common burdens. If there should be a closer inquiry into other forms of property than the real estate, taxation could be more equitably distributed and more exact justice could be done to all citizens alike— which is indeed the highest duty of a state government."

THE LISTING SYSTEM.

A law requiring the listing of property by the tax payer under oath, and generally referred to as the "Vermont system," appears to be considered in this State as a radical innovation, something peculiar to Vermont; but the fact is, such a system prevails in a large number of the states. Some features of the Vermont tax laws are new, but its central principle, that of requiring the tax payer to render to the assessors an inventory on oath of all his taxable property, is almost as old as the tax systems of the country. That it may appear how general is this requirement, we subjoin a reference to the assessment laws of most of the states.

MASSACHUSETTS—In this state the assessors are required to notify the inhabitants to bring in lists of their taxable polls and personal estate, and may or may not require real estate to be included in the lists, and in all cases shall require persons bringing in lists to make oath to the same, and a false list subjects the lister to a fine of not exceeding $1,000, or imprisonment not more than one year. The valuation is made as of the first day of May of each year.

CONNECTICUT—Assessors must require residents to bring in lists of property owned by them on the first day of each October, and to make oath that said lists are true and that the lister has not conveyed, transferred nor concealed any property to evade taxation. Neglect or refusal to present and swear to such lists subjects the tax payer to an addition of ten per cent to such valuation as the assessors may prepare from the best of their information and belief.

NEW HAMPSHIRE—Blank inventories are furnished by the Secretary of State to inhabitants through the assessors in proper form and to contain suitable interrogatories to fully meet the requirements of law, so arranged and formulated as to require under oath full information of the person or corporation to be taxed, of the classes in gross and the amount thereof of each class of his real and personal property and the value, by such classes, of his personal property liable to be taxed, and such further information as will enable the assessors to assess such property at its true value. Assessors must make up lists of property for all who fail or refuse to furnish or swear to said lists, and then assess such delinquent four times as much as otherwise would have been taxable to such person. False oath declared perjury and punishable accordingly.

OHIO—Assessors must furnish all residents with blank lists to be filled out in detail with an inventory of their taxable property, sworn to and returned to the assessors within ten days. The statements required are very minute, must include both real and personal property with value, but the assessors are not bound by such value. Persons claiming not to own property are requested to make oath to that effect.

ILLINOIS—By an amendment in 1879, a list of property in detail must be returned to the assessors on oath by the tax payer. Refusal or neglect to return such list on oath or the return of a false list incurs a doomage of fifty per cent of entire valuation. Any person who shall refuse, neglect or fail to return required list is guilty of misdemeanor and shall be fined not exceeding $200. Assessors may compel the attendance of any person for examination on oath, whom they suppose to have knowledge of amount and value of the property under consideration.

PENNSYLVANIA—Assessors must make up the lists of persons and property from the best information obtainable. No oath is required of the tax payer, but the assessor is subject to fine and imprisonment for intentionally undervaluing or omitting to value and assess any taxable property. This is for local assessments. By act of 1889, all persons holding moneys, notes, mortgages, accounts bearing interest, stocks, bonds, &c., must return on oath to assessors a list of such property to be taxed for the state three mills on the dollar.

NEW YORK—The method of assessment is the same as in Pennsylvania. No list or oath is required of the tax payer.

MARYLAND—Instead of requiring the tax payer to list or disclose on oath the amount and value of his property as in most of the states is required, Maryland takes the opposite and, perhaps equally effective method, of requiring the assessors to hunt up taxable property with the utmost diligence, proceeding on the principle that every man is to be taxed for

2

all he had the year before and as much more as the assessors can in the meantime dig out.

The assessment is really made by the County Commissioners, who assess the tax according to the last year's valuation, with such additions as the assessors have since returned. That is to say, when a man is once assessed for any kind of property, he is forever after taxed for the same unless he takes pains to satisfy the County Commissioners that he has sold or otherwise disposed of the same, and at the same time must satisfactorily explain what has become of the proceeds of such sale and otherwise make full disclosure of his property.

By this method of continually hunting up all acquisitions of property and, at the same time, continuing to tax all property ever owned by the tax payer until he volunteers a sworn statement, Maryland without requiring a sworn list virtually drives the tax payer to submit to examination under oath to protect himself.

Registers of Wills, Clerk of Courts and Commissioner of the Land Office are required to make return to the County Commissioners of the several counties, giving information of taxable property found on the records of their respective offices.

IOWA—Assessors must require a list from the tax payer of all his property and shall require him to swear to it. In default of such sworn list, it is mandatory upon the assessors to fix the valuation of such person's property, from the best information obtainable, and then double it.

MICHIGAN—The assessors are not obliged to require sworn lists from tax payers, but may do so, and may summon and examine any person on oath whom they may believe has information of the possessions of the delinquent.

WISCONSIN—Assessors must require lists on oath from the tax payer, and neglect to require it subjects the assessor to a penalty of from $100 to $300. A false statement in list subjects the lister to forfeiture of ten dollars in every hundred or fraction of a hundred dollars withheld from his list.

VERMONT—Blanks for inventories of taxable property are prepared by the Secretary of State and distributed by the listers and clerks of towns to the inhabitants and to non-resident tax payers by mail. The blanks contain questions calling for a minute detail of the taxable property of the tax payer, real and personal and debts payable and receivable and the inventory must be signed, sworn to and returned to the town listers. In case of neglect or refusal to return sworn list, the listers are required to ascertain from the best information obtainable the amount and value of the property which should have been listed and then to double the value for taxation, and the delinquent has no appeal. False oath to list is perjury and punished accordingly. If a lister accepts a list of property not properly filled out or sworn to, or for neglect to appraise each item, he is liable to a fine of $200 for the town.

KANSAS—Every person is required to return list of taxable property and value it, on blanks furnished by assessors. Persons claiming not to own taxable property must so state on the list and return it under oath to the assessors. Persons returning lists of property need not verify it by oath unless so required by the assessors. The assessors are not bound by the lists.

MINNESOTA—A list must be returned to the assessors, giving a full and detailed statement of property on oath. Blanks provided by state. No penalty for neglect to return such list is provided, but the assessors may make up the valuation of the delinquent from their best information.

CALIFORNIA—Assessors must exact from every tax payer a full and detailed list of property on oath in writing. Assessors may summon and examine witnesses in regard to the statements filed by any person. If none returned, the assessors may make valuation from their best information and belief, and no appeal is allowed.   Property concealed or misrepresented by owner to avoid taxation, on discovery must be assessed at not exceeding ten times its real value, and no appeal.

NEW JERSEY—Lists required in detail of ratable property. Neglect or false return subjects to a double valuation, with no remedy except on proof before County Commissioners that there was no culpable neglect or fraud.

RHODE ISLAND—List must be returned on oath, but the only penalty for neglect or refusal is forfeiture of all right of appeal or other remedy if overtaxed.

VIRGINIA—List must be returned on oath under penalty of from $30 to $1,000 for neglect or refusal to make sworn return.   No assessor shall receive a list not sworn to, under penalty of $500.   By act of 1887, it is provided that in case of failure to return on oath all bonds, notes or other evidences of debt by any person, bank or firm, they shall not be recoverable in any action at law or in equity in the courts of the state, until tax is paid, and 50 per cent. per annum from the time the tax accrued.

WEST VIRGINIA—List must be returned on oath, under penalty, for neglect or refusal, of from $10 to $100, and a forfeiture of five per cent. of the valuation of all property omitted, to go to the informer.

OREGON—List must be made on oath, under penalty, for neglect, of $20 fine.

MISSOURI—List must be returned on oath.   Neglect or refusal subjects the tax payer to a fine of not exceeding $1,000, and forfeiture of right of appeal.

GEORGIA—A constitutional provision in this state makes a tax defaulter ineligible to a seat in the legislature.   No oath is required to list.

KENTUCKY—List must be returned on oath.   Neglect or refusal incurs a fine of $100 and treble taxation.   County Attorney must enforce the fine.

SOUTH CAROLINA—A list on oath is required with very minute statement. Refusal to swear is contempt, punishable by imprisonment. Property omitted from list must be added with 50 per cent. additional.

ARKANSAS—A very detailed statement is required of the tax payer on oath or affirmation. Wilful omission is made a misdemeanor, punishable with a fine of not exceeding $100, *and* imprisonment not more than three months. It is made the duty of the assessors and prosecuting officers to bring offenders against these provisions to trial. The assessors are bound under penalty of a fine not exceeding $50 for each offence, to require sworn inventories of taxable property.

That this plan of requiring sworn inventories of taxable property is open to the objection of being inquisitorial is undeniable, but it is difficult to conceive of any method of assessment of general property that is not more or less inquisitorial. It is doubtless much more agreeable to have no questions asked—no attempt made by the assessors to find one's property for entry on his lists—but that method has been often tried with very unsatisfactory results. Indeed, it is on account of its insufficiency that the legislature is trying, through this Commission, to devise a better one. That the state has a right to demand this scrutiny into the affairs of the people, if just and equal taxation require it, there can be no question; yet, there should be no needless exposure of private business and property to the public. We have made provision for protection of this kind in the bill. The inventories returned by the tax payers are not open to public inspection, and the assessors must not disclose their contents, being under penalties if they do, excepting to a few designated officers if necessary in the prosecution of violations of the act.

This is not a new feature, even in Maine. The law in all cases directs that the assessors *may* require the lister to make oath, and it imposes a penalty for the non-production of an inventory, by depriving the tax payer of the right of appeal if unjustly taxed or over-assessed. If these provisions are just and salutary in their weakness, we believe they will prove much more so by being made strong and mandatory. The proposed law is not, therefore, an innovation, but the making prominent and potent of measures which our tax laws have always contained in a diluted and inefficient form. The bitterest antagonists of such required returns of property are invariably those who wish to avoid a fair and full assessment of their property; who, having long escaped paying their just share of taxes, desire to perpetuate their exemptions, and shift the burden they can easily bear upon the shoulders of their neighbors whose property may be open and visible to the assessor. From such objectors is sure to come the attempt to arouse public sentiment against such a law by alleging that it is inquisitorial, and an obnoxious intermeddling with private affairs. Let those whose property is in land, houses, farms, stock and other forms of visible property, see to it that those who unfairly escape, may, by the only feasible mode which law can provide under our Constitution, be compelled to bear their own just portion of the tax load.

RESULTS OF THE LISTING SYSTEM.

We have endeavored to find what has been the result elsewhere of the practical application of this method of getting at property for the purpose of taxation. Theory is one thing; practical tests are often apt to show quite another thing; especially is this true of theory and practice in the matter of taxation. We have, therefore, selected three states in which the "inquisitorial" method is most specific and searching, and three states in which there is little or no attempt to hold the tax payers to any accountability in respect to disclosing their property to the assessors. If in the one case it shall be found that personal and intangible property is made to bear with more equality its share of the public burdens, as compared with real and tangible property, than in the other case, it will be an argument of weight in favor of the method under which such a result is produced.

The three states having the "listing-under-oath" method which we will select are Ohio, New Hampshire and Vermont, and the three having most nearly an opposite method : New York, Michigan and Maryland.*

The following table shows the last valuations of real and personal estate in the states named, for purposes of taxation, the aggregates and the percentage of the personal to the whole valuation :

	Real.	Personal.	Aggregate.	Per cent of Personal.
Ohio,	$1,173,106,705	$515,569,463	$1,688,676,168	30 5
N. Hampshire,	120,629,345	61,983,716	182,613,061	33.9
Vermont,	110.385,754	49,880.623	160.266,376	31.1
New York,	3,213,171, 201	354,258.556	3,567,429,757	9.6
Michigan,	432,861,884	84,804,475	517.666.359	16.4
Maryland,	368,442,913	128.864,762	497,307,675	25 8

NEW HAMPSHIRE.

The assessment law of New Hampshire as amended by the legislature in 1879, requires inventories on oath from all tax payers filled out in detail, and a wilful neglect or refusal subjects the delinquent to a doomage of four times the amount he would otherwise be legally taxed. False swearing to list is made perjury. The penalty is regarded in the state as too severe and serves often to defeat its object. Assessors cannot be made to assess a full legal tax on a person's property and then quadruple it. For that reason the law fails to accomplish what it might otherwise accomplish.

We visited Portsmouth and Concord to investigate the practical workings of the law. The fact that the personal property amounts to thirty-four per cent of the aggregate valuation of the state, exclusive of deposits in the savings banks, is pretty conclusive evidence as to the effectiveness of

*NOTE—The Maryland Tax Commission has recommended a law requiring lists to be returned by tax payers subject to examination on oath and penalty of imprisonment not less than one nor more than ten years for false returns.

In Michigan a new law was enacted at the recent session of its legislature, making more exacting provision for return of lists on oath and providing that, in case of failure by a tax payer to make such return of his property, the supervisors may examine "any other person or persons" as to the value of the delinquent's property. This would appear to be a step backward to the ancient Rhode Island system of getting one's valuation from his neighbors.

the system.   From Hon. John M. Hill of Concord, Chairman of
the State Board of Equalization, we gained much information
about the practical results of the inventory method of assessment.   He assured us that its operation was most satisfactory and had brought to the notice of the assessors much personal property, especially bonds, notes, cash and other forms
of intangible assets that had before escaped.   The money on
hand and at interest in 1889 which was inventoried amounted
to $7,920,348.   And this is in spite of the fact stated in the
report of the Equalizing Board in 1887, as follows :

"The commissioners having been requested by the Board
to ascertain how generally individual inventories were sworn
to, report that they generally were sworn to, yet, in one large
county in three towns only was it done, and, in another large
county, only in about half of the towns."

This failure to make oath was believed by the officials
whom we consulted, to be due to the neglect of assessors in
these towns to enforce the quadruple doomage.   It was
believed if the penalty were but half as severe, the law would
be better enforced.   The law is handicapped by its severity,
yet its general result is beneficial.

THE VERMONT LISTING LAW.

The present tax law of Vermont was enacted in 1880.
The last assessment of real estate before the law was passed
was in 1876.   It is interesting to compare with this the various state valuations since this law, known as the grand list
law, has been in force.

In 1876 the total assessed valuation of real and personal
property of the state was $99,717,603.

In 1889 it was $160,847,357, an increase of $61,029,754.

The personal property of the state in 1880, just before the
passage of the grand list law, was assessed at $15,370,152
and the real estate $71,436,623, total $86,806.775, the personal property being less than 17 per cent of the aggregate.
In 1886, the valuation of personal property had arisen to
$49,927,597 or more than 200 per cent increase above the

valuation of 1876, while the real estate had increased but 38 per cent.

A correspondent writing from St. Albans, giving a detailed statement of the finances of Vermont, says: "A comparison of the assessed valuation of real and personal property in 1876 and 1889 in this state shows a very large increase during this period. It should not be forgotten that the additions to the grand list since 1876, by new buildings, improved real estate and industrial development have been very extensive. The grand list was also largely increased by the new grand list law of 1880, which resulted in the assessment of a large amount of personal property that had hitherto escaped taxation."

This statement we found fully corroborated by the testimony of state officials and others in Montpelier and Burlington. Lieutenant Governor Woodbury informed us that in Burlington the assessed valuation of property was nearly doubled in one year after the law went into effect, the increase being chiefly in personal property. In 1886 the assessed valuation of personal property in Burlington was about 42 per cent of the total valuation.

Contrary to what we had been led to believe, we found that the Vermont grand list law is very popular among the tax payers. We interviewed many business men and consulted the assessors of several cities. While for a year or two the "prying" qualities of the statute were somewhat distasteful, when it was found that "all were served alike" and that the tax rate went down as the aggregate valuation of property went up, the law was accepted and acquiesced in as, on the whole, very beneficial to the state at large.

This grand list law is not the only reformation Vermont has made in its tax laws recently. In 1882 the legislature passed a corporation tax law which was designed to yield revenues enough for all the state expenses which had before been derived from a general tax on polls and property. It provided for a direct assessment upon the business done in

the state by railroad, insurance, guarantee, express, telegraph, telephone and transportation companies and savings
banks and trust companies. This law took effect in 1883.
While the taxes yielded by assessments under this act
amounted to $250,000 in 1889, the state found it necessary to
levy a tax of two mills on the dollar upon property, amounting to $353,412. It will evidently be some time before the
state can dispense with a property tax for state purposes.
The effect of the grand list law is very clearly seen when the
rate of state taxation before and after its passage are compared. For the three years immediately preceding its passage the rate averaged three and one-third mills on the dollar.
While for the three years succeeding its passage, and before
the corporation tax act took effect, the average rate was but
one and a half mills.

If it is inquired : "Has not this inquisitorial and oath-com-
pelling law driven property out of the state?" we are able
to reply that we have found no evidence of it. We made
special inquiry as to this point. While much money is being
invested in Western speculations—in which particular Vermont is like all the rest of New England—there has been no
loss of property or of business, so far as we could learn, by
reason of the new system of taxation.

EQUALIZATION.

Governor Bodwell, in his address to the legislature, in January, 1887, called its attention to the need of an improved
system for equalizing the valuation of the State, as follows :

"It should be made the steady aim of the Legislative
power of the state to equalize the burdens of government.
To that end I recommend that an earnest inquiry be made
into the mode of our valuation, with the view to its improvement. A board, composed of one commissioner from each
county, hastily summoned at the close of each decade, with
each member naturally endeavoring to have his own county
valued at as low a rate as possible, would not seem to be the
best method devisable. And yet, that is the character of our
present system. A smaller number of commissioners, say

not exceeding three, at work for a longer period, chosen, not as the representatives of the counties in which they may reside, but for the whole state, would be less cumbrous, less expensive and in many ways more efficient. The systems of valuation in force in other New England states should be carefully examined. Some improved methods in tho-e states could, I have reason to believe, be profitably incorporated in our own system."

Many petitions were presented to the legislature of that year, asking for legislation which should make taxation more equal. Nothing, however, was accomplished. It is obviously impossible for any committee of the legislature, in the hurry of a brief session, to make such a study of the subject as to enable them to agree upon any important changes in the system, such as the request in these petitions involved.

In his inaugural address, in January, 1889, Governor Burleigh cogently exposed some of the evils of the present mode of equalizing the valuation of the State. He said :

"It will be your duty to provide for the valuation of the property of the State which is required by our Constitution 'at least once in ten years.' It doubtless gives greater satis-faction to have a board composed of one representative from each county, and I therefore recommend that the board of valuation be thus constituted. In some respects, however, evil results have followed from the zealous and yet proper care taken, that no section shall be taxed more than its fair share of the public burdens. Each county sedulously guard-ing its own interests and securing as low a valuation as pos-sible, the result has been that the aggregate official valuation of the State has been far below its real value. In this respect the State of Maine has not been presented to the country in as strong a financial position as she is entitled to hold. We negotiated our war loans on a valuation of one hundred and sixty-two millions of dollars, and if it had been really believed that that sum represented the actual wealth of the State, we could not have so readily placed an aggregate loan that amounted to five per cent of our total property. The valuation taken by the United States Census comes nearer doing us perfect justice than the valuation taken by the State, for in 1870, when the State Board of Valuation said Maine was worth $225,000,000, the United States Census fixed the valuation at $348,000,000. In 1880, when the

State government said Maine was worth $236,000,000 the United States census fixed the valuation at $511,000,000.

"If the incredulous may think the last figures of the United States Census were too high those best acquainted with the extent of our resources and of our recent development in many directions will agree that it is very much nearer the actual amount of the property in Maine in 1880 than is given in our own valuation."

Governor Plaisted urged upon the attention of the legislature of 1881, the necessity of more frequent readjustments of the valuation of the State. In his address to the legislature he said :

"This equalization of the public burdens so devoutly to be wished and so earnestly to be sought is a subject that should command your especial attention. Without the determination of values for the purpose of taxation, there can be no equalization of the public burdens. Values should be readjusted oftener than once in ten years. State boards of equalization, or tax commissioners have been created in many states of the Union, for the determination and readjustment of values and the discovery of new sources of revenue for purposes of taxation."

EQUALIZATION IN OTHER STATES.

The methods adopted to keep valuations equalized in many of the leading states are here given :

MASSACHUSETTS—The treasurer is *ex-officio*, tax commissioner. A deputy tax commissioner who has charge of the whole work reports to the General Court on equalization and apportionment and the number of polls every third year. The deputy tax commissioner is also commissioner of corporations. Returns of local assessors are made to him, also returns of corporations, from which he prepares abstracts and makes up the apportionments.

NEW HAMPSHIRE—The legislature makes apportionment and equalization every fourth year, on report of the state board of equalization, consisting of five members appointed by the supreme judicial court and commissioned by the governor. Inventories of property are returned to the secretary

of state annually by selectmen of towns and by county commissioners quadrennially. The county commissioners constitute a board of equalization for each county and are required
once in four years to visit every town in their county and
personally inspect property subject to taxation and equalize
values. One member of each county board with the state
board constitutes a joint board of equalization.

CONNECTICUT—The state treasurer and comptroller constitute the state board of equalization. They equalize the
assessment lists of the towns every year. Upon their return
of valuation, the state taxes are apportioned.

VERMONT—City and town "Listers" make up lists of taxable property and polls and return the same to their respective
town clerks on or before April 15, yearly. Town clerks prepare in form prescribed by law, abstracts of lists and return
the same to the secretary of state before July 1, yearly. And
from these abstracts the secretary of state (having reference
to equalizing board in "quadrennial" years) makes up the
state list, which is the basis for the apportionment of the
state tax. Town listers to return new appraisal of real estate,
every four years. The county equalization conventions, made
up of one lister from each town in the county, meet in the
shire towns of their respective counties in August in the year
of quadrennial appraisal, and average the valuations and
return corrected lists to the secretary of state. The state
equalizing board, made up of one member from each county
convention, meets on the third Tuesday of August of quadrennial year, and makes report and transmits the same through
the secretary of state to the legislature on the second Monday
of October. This valuation, after approval by the legislature
and with such corrections as are by law authorized to be made
from year to year, is to stand for four years.

KANSAS—The assessors of the several towns in each county
meet in their respective shire towns annually on the first
Monday of March and agree upon an equal basis for valua-

tion of property. The county commissioners of each county, constituting a board of equalization for their respective counties, meet annually, on the first Monday of June, and equalize the value of real property. Clerk of court forwards to state auditor an abstract of the assessment roll of real property and of certain personal property. The state board of equalization, consisting of the secretary of state, auditor and treasurer, with power to appoint assistants, meets each year, on the second Wednesday of July and apportions and equalizes the state tax among the several counties.

Iowa—The executive council constitutes the state board of equalization, and meets in July of each year in which real estate is assessed. This board equalizes from abstracts returned by county boards. The county boards of equalization consisting of the county supervisors, meet in their respective counties each year in June, and equalize the assessments of the several towns in their respective counties. The town boards of equalization consist of the township trustees.

Minnesota—County boards of equalization, consisting of the county commissioners, or a majority of them, and county auditor, equalize all valuations in their respective counties from returns of towns. The state board of equalization consisting of the governor, state auditor and attorney general, with one qualified elector from each judicial district, appointed by the governor, with consent of the senate, meets annually to equalize state valuation.

Michigan—The state board of equalization, consisting of the lieutenant governor, auditor general, secretary of state, state revenue commissioner and land officer, meet periodically for purpose of equalizing the state taxes.

Illinois—State board of equalization, consisting of one member from each congressional district, and elected by the people every fourth year, with power to appoint assistants, equalize valuations and apportion state taxes every year.

PENNSYLVANIA—Equalization board, called revenue commissioners, consisting of auditor general, state treasurer and secretary of state, meet triennially. The county commissioners of the several counties return to the board aggregates of all taxable property as returned to them by town assessors. The revenue commissioners then equalize "as far as possible to make all taxes bear equally upon all property in the commonwealth in proportion to its actual value."

NEW YORK—There are three state assessors appointed by governor, who with the commissioner of the land office, constitute a state board of equalization. This board equalizes the valuation of the state annually. The state assessors must visit each county once in two years and prepare statistics and facts relating to the value of property of all kinds.

WISCONSIN—The town board of review consisting of supervisors, clerk and assessors of cities and the president, clerk and assessors of villages, meets annually on last Monday of June, for purpose of equalization, and constitute a board of appeal. Town boards make return of aggregates to county clerk, who in turn transmits abstract to secretary of state. The state board of equalization, consisting of secretary of state, treasurer and attorney general, meets annually, and equalizes values preparatory to assessing state tax. County board equalizes annually as basis of county tax.

CALIFORNIA—The state board of equalization consisting of the comptroller (*ex-officio*) and two other members appointed by the governor, and provided with a clerk, equalizes biennially. State board of equalization may fix the rate of state tax in the absence of action by county board of supervisors whose powers under the California code are very large. The latter equalize annually for county purposes and every county tax not exceeding one per cent of valuation. For taxation purposes, the county is the unit.

By act of 1889, the state board of equalization is charged with the duty of assessing railroads.

The following states also have boards of equalization: Arizona, Colorado, Idaho, Nebraska, North Dakota, South Dakota and Wyoming.

Ohio is the only state, we think, besides Maine, in which the valuation is equalized but once in ten years. In his annual message, January, 1887, Governor Foraker said:

"The last decennial appraisement of real estate (1880) was had at a period of great prosperity, it was a time of high values; since then there has been a heavy decline; farm property is from twenty-five to fifty per cent. cheaper to-day than it was then. * * * * · * The valuations placed upon the real estate of these cities (certain large cities of the state) are in the aggregate fifty per cent of their true value in money, and, in some cases will not exceed twenty-five per cent."

Thus were the depreciating farm lands made to pay more and the rising city lands less than their share of taxes for a portion, at least, of the decade. Precisely the same thing has occurred in Maine as will be seen by a glance at the table in the appendix.

That table was made up before the report of the valuation commission for 1890 was made, and shows an increase since 1880 of $30,880,069 in valuation of the state, including wild lands. This increase, however, was in eleven counties only, while in five counties there was a decrease in value of $2,481,-320. It is clear that for a portion of the ten years the five losing counties, farming counties in every instance, have been paying more than their share of state and county taxes, and that the eleven counties making the gains, counties in which the cities are situated, have been paying less. In other words, burdens belonging to the prosperous and wealthy counties to carry have been placed by this system of decennial equalization, upon the counties which are growing poorer. This $30,000,000 of increase at two and one-fourth mills on the dollar, the present tax rate. would have yielded the State $67,500 per year. Or taking $3,000,000 as the average yearly increase for the ten years, the tax on it would have averaged $33,500 per year, which other property has unjustly been obliged to pay, aggregating for the whole period $335,000.

STATE ASSESSORS.

The want of a central supervising head to our tax system we would supply by having a state board of assessors whose duties shall include among others, the general oversight of the state revenues, the assessment of such corporations as pay taxes directly to the state, the formulating and preparation of blank lists for returns of tax payers to the local assessors; the inventories of assessors; blank books for annual return of aggregates by local to state assessors; the apportionment of state taxes voted by the legislature and the enforcement of taxes, delinquent, upon wild lands and in unincorporated places. A not less important function of the state assessors in the plan we recommend, is that of state board of equalization. It is made their duty to equalize the valuation of the state biennially, in order that taxes voted by each legislature may be assessed on a new valuation, as it actually exists at the time of the assessment. It will also be the province and duty of the state assessors to preserve and report tabulated statistics of taxation and valuation of the different classes of property in the state, which have never been heretofore kept. In respect to such statistics, our archives are singularly deficient. Nothing of our valuation has been officially preserved excepting the decennial valuation in the aggregate by towns, of the valuation commissioners. And these do not distinguish between real and personal property. The resolves under which they have been appointed from time to time have not required anything more than aggregate valuations and polls to be reported. There is no record of the amount and value of personal property or of real estate separately assessed; and no data whatever from which may be learned the progress or regress of the state or of any county or section of it in the amount and value of the several classes of assessable property; of the cattle, horses, buildings, stocks, mortgages, money at interest, ships and vessels, stocks in trade and the like. Such statistics for the last few decades

would have been very serviceable to us in ascertaining what
property, and to what extent, has escaped its share of taxation, and to what extent the law, the assessors or the collectors have been responsible.

No state, we think, is so much remiss in this respect as
ours.   A letter to the secretary of state of any state from
which we have desired statements in detail of valuations, has
brought the information in reports of auditors, comptrollers,
state assessors, tax commissioners or equalization boards,
while we have called in vain upon the records of our own
State for much needed data, whereby comparative research
could be made.

Thus constituting the state assessors an equalizing board
will insure a more frequent equalization of values by officials
who would be independent of local influences.   Such a change
has long been urged upon the legislature by successive governors, and we believe is generally demanded throughout the
state as promising a substantial measure of relief.

The plan embodied in the bill is to have three state assessors, to be appointed by the governor with the confirmation
of the council.   It appears to us reasonable and proper that
a board vested with such powers and duties should be removed
as far as possible from the suspicion of partizanship, and made
as independent of party as our system of government will
permit.   We recommend therefore, and so provide in the
bill, that one of the associate members must be taken from
each of the leading political parties.   That the knowledge
and experience gained by these officials may be utilized for
the state their term of office is fixed at six years and the term
of but one is to expire the same year.

The office, it will be readily seen, is no sinecure.   It
requires the highest order of ability, intelligence and character.   Such men as are necessary to fill the position with the
greatest benefit to the people cannot be found for small pay.
The salary must be in some degree commensurate with the
important service required.   The sums named in the bill as
salaries are certainly as small as will secure the talent required.

The cost to the state directly of making such equalization as can be made under our present system in a single year is $16,000. It is impossible to estimate the cost to towns for sending officials and counsel to Augusta to secure lower valuations but it must amount in the aggregate to thousands. Massachusetts pays its deputy tax commissioner a salary of $2,750 and to his assistants in the aggregate, about $67,000 more, annually. New Jersey has four state assessors at a salary of $2,500 each and expenses. Maryland pays her tax commissioner $2,500 a year and travelling expenses to the amount of $800. In none of these cases do the officers also have to perform the duties of an equalizing board. The duties of the state assessors will certainly not be less onerous or important to the public than are those of the railroad commissioners the amount of whose compensation is the same as we suggest in the bill for the state assessors.*

INCOME TAXES.

Many theorists, in the discussion of the tax problem, advocate an income tax as the fairest form of taxation. In theory there is much to sustain it. In practice it is almost universally a failure. In theory it seems just that a person should be taxed upon the net yield of his occupation or investments the best gauge of his taxable ability, but in the levying of such a tax it has always been found that art, subterfuge, evasion and downright perjury have rendered the system inefficient and futile. To tax capital, property, lands and also the income arising from their employment is intolerable as double taxation; to exempt such property and rely on the income from them alone leaves open a hundred ways for evasion and is

*Note—The Special Tax Commission of Connecticut forcibly recommend a permanent tax commission for that state. They say in their Report to the General Assembly: "We believe that the time has now come when such a measure must be adopted in order to make our tax system accomplish its design. The additional expense attached to the creation of a new office, will, we are confident, be repaid many fold to the state itself by the increase of revenue which may fairly be anticipated from the general supervision over its assessment and collection to be received by the tax commissioner, while the adjustment of the state taxes between the towns can hardly fail to be made with more fairness and equality."

open to grave objections as being in conflict with the constitutional provision requiring that all property shall be taxed according to its just value. It has been tried in several states, but has proved unsatisfactory in all, and it is a potent argument against this form of taxation, that in the efforts that have been made in most states of the Union, during the past ten years, to find new sources of revenue, there has been so little disposition to resort to income taxes. In North Carolina, by act of 1889, a tax of one per cent was laid on incomes derived from property not otherwise taxed, and of one-half of one per cent on salaries and fees allowing the individual returning his income to deduct $1000 for family expenses. Virginia has a general income tax law, but judging from its results to the revenue of the state it appears to be much "more honored in the breach than in the observance," as only about $16,000 is realized from the tax on incomes in a year. Massachusetts nominally taxes "so much of the income from a profession, trade or employment as exceeds the sum of $2000 a year," but according to the assessors' lists the number of individuals whose incomes exceed that sum is surprisingly small. The only other state, in whose revenue system the income tax is a feature, is Pennsylvania, where a special tax is levied on the income of private bankers and brokers.

Writers on taxation who are most opposed to taxes on general property are not agreed as to the justness or feasibility of income taxes. Judge Cooley vigorously opposes this form of taxation as follows : "Income taxes are inquisitorial and teach evasion and fraud. No means at the command of government has ever enabled it to arrive, with anything like accuracy, at the incomes of its citizens. They resist in all practicable modes, not only because they desire to avoid the public burdens which they are certain are not equally imposed, but also because they are not willing that their private affairs be exposed to the public." It is as difficult to apply such a tax in this age as it was in Rome under the Empire when torture was applied by the assessors to ascertain the profits of employments.

We have seen this form of taxation advocated by well meaning writers as being in the interest of farmers. If it were practicable to get at all incomes for taxation, the farmer would be benefited as all other classes would be by the consequent lessening of general property taxes, but, under the practical workings of such a method, the farmer would be placed at great disadvantage and put to much vexatious labor. It would not only become necessary for him to keep strict account of his receipts and expenses but also the value of the farm products consumed on the farm, for such products would assuredly be a part of his income applied toward the support of his family.

In view of the facts above stated, we have not thought it advisable to include an income tax in the system herewith proposed. Clergymen, professors of colleges, clerks and salaried officers, could thus be reached quite effectively doubtless, but it is not thought that it is required that these should be singled out for a special mode of taxation, especially as many have houses or other taxable property in which their incomes, above the cost of living, is invested.

THE TAX ASSESSOR.

Whatever system of taxation may be adopted, the responsibility for its efficient and just operation must rest largely upon the assessors. They are to fix the values and upon their activity and faithfulness, in a good degree, depends the bringing to light much property for purposes of taxation that would otherwise escape. The assessor, above all other town officials, should possess the attributes of intelligence, sound judgment and courage. He should be a man who cannot be bribed or cajoled from the strict line of his duty, to "assess all property equally and according to the just value thereof," as required by the imperative mandate of the Constitution.

There is no more responsible officer under our town system of government, the whole fabric of which may be said to rest and its institutions to operate through and by its system of revenues. Recognizing the vital importance of sound and sure provisions for securing revenue, the national government protects the raising and collection of them with the safeguards of its severest penal laws, and the evasion of a tax duly imposed by the government incurs the penalty of heavy forfeitures, fines or imprisonment. The revenue laws of the United States exact the most scrupulous observance of its provisions, not only as to the individual who would evade payment of his dues, but as to the officer whose duty it is to enforce it. The state laws should be equally peremptory in holding revenue officers to strict fidelity in their enforcement. Our Maine assessors are unquestionably as able and efficient as any and the fault is largely in the looseness of the tax law. Yet it has long been the custom of assessors to ignore the explicit requirement of the Constitution of the State above quoted. Property is assessed at much less than its just value in many towns. It is very common for assessors to value real estate at three-fourths, two-thirds and even one-half its true value. In the late returns of the assessors of all the towns of the State for the use of the State Valuation Commissioners it appears that the assessors of 132 towns based their taxes on less than "a just value" of the property assessed. Thirteen based them on four-fifths value, thirty-five on three-fourths value, fifty-three on two-thirds value, and sixteen on one-half, while in two towns the assessors considered their duty done when they assessed at one-third of the "cash value" of the property taxed.

It has been our purpose to make the assessor the important and responsible officer that he should be under our system and yet to make him the executor and servant of the law, and not its superior. The proposed law, therefore, leaves but little discretion in his hands. It points the way and commands him to follow under severe penalties for neglect or misfeasance. It holds him rigidly to a just valuation with no discretion to construe that to mean a *half* value, and is equally explicit in forbidding any intentional under-valuation or over-valuation in any case or for any purpose whatever. With all the assessors in the State doing their duties promptly, faithfully and all alike under the general supervision of a board of State assessors held, by provisions of equal explicitness, to fidelity and vigilance, a nearer approach to equality and hence a lessening of the rate of taxation may be confidently looked for.

As a measure towards making assessors independent of local circumstances, we recommend a change in the law providing for their election and tenure of office in towns having more than two thousand inhabitants and submit herewith a bill which provides that in such towns the selectmen shall not be assessors and that assessors shall hold office for three years, one going out each year, if there are three, and one or two as their terms expire, if five are chosen. This method, it is believed, will insure experience as well as independence, to a greater degree than the present method of yearly rotation of the whole board and a mixture of the duties of selectmen and assessors in the same persons.

POLL TAXES.

Under our present statute, a poll tax of not exceeding three dollars is assessable upon every male inhabitant above the age of twenty-one years (with certain exemptions) for state, county and town purposes, and an equal sum may be assessed on each poll for highway expenses. This makes it possible for towns to assess six dollars, in all, as a poll tax. There is great variety in the poll tax laws of the several states. Some states have abolished the poll tax entirely. Some make its payment a prerequisite to the right to vote.

MASSACHUSETTS imposes a poll tax of $1.00 on male citizens above twenty years of age and fifty cents on females of voting age who ask to be taxed in order to exercise their limited right of suffrage. State and county taxes only assessed on polls. No town or highway poll taxes.

NEW HAMPSHIRE—All male poles from twenty-one to seventy years of age, except paupers and insane persons, are taxed. The tax must be equal to the tax on $100 of valuation of property in the town where the poll is taxed. Disabled soldiers of the late war may be exempted, in the discretion of the selectmen.

VERMONT taxes two dollars on all polls of male inhabitants, citizens and aliens, with exemption of persons actually poor and soldiers who lost an arm, leg or eye-sight in the war. Members of the militia or of fire companies may be exempted if towns so vote.

CONNECTICUT—The poll tax is one dollar and no more for town and state purposes, and school districts may tax at the same rate as $100 value of property is taxed by the district. A great many exemptions of the poll tax are provided for ; students, members of fire companies, active members of militia companies, and soldiers who served three months in the late war, ministers, priests, paupers, idiots, lunatics and indigent, sick and infirm persons and persons above seventy years of age. Every able bodied person is required to work by himself or substitute at least one day on the highway, commutable at twelve and a half cents an hour.

PENNSYLVANIA restricts its poll taxes to persons holding offices and posts of profit, professions, trades, occupations and single free men, above the age of twenty-one years who shall follow no trade, occupation or calling. It is unlimited for state and county purposes, and for school purposes not less than fifty cents.

Section 1 of Art. 8 of the Constitution of Pennsylvania requires as a qualification to vote, that the citizen shall, if twenty-two years of age or upward, have paid a state or county tax assessed within two years, and paid at least one month before election. By joint resolution the legislature has this year submitted to the people a proposed amendment, doing away with this requirement of the Constitution. (Laws of 1889, p. 439.)

OHIO—The poll tax in this state is fixed in amount to two days' labor on the highway and is commutable at $3.00. It is imposed on all males between twenty-one and fifty-five years of age. The exemptions are disabled soldiers pensioned by the United States and members of fire companies serving without pay.

ILLINOIS has no poll tax law.

KANSAS—Municipal corporations having less than 15,000 inhabitants may impose a poll tax of not exceeding $1.00 on male inhabitants over twenty-one years of age. Active members of fire companies are exempt.

CALIFORNIA—Every male inhabitant between the ages of twenty-one and sixty must pay a poll tax of $2.00. The exempts are officers, musicians and privates of the national guard, while doing military service, and all who have served for seven consecutive years. A highway poll tax of two days' labor on roads, commutable at $4.00 or at such rate not exceeding that amount as the assessors may fix, is also provided.

MINNESOTA—The poll tax law is as follows : "It shall be lawful for the Common Council of cities of above 2,000 inhabitants, to levy at any time a corporation poll tax upon every qualified voter, not exceeding $2.00 a year."

WISCONSIN — Every male inhabitant between twenty-one and fifty years of age must pay a poll tax of $1.50 for highway purposes. The exempts are disabled soldiers of the late war, paupers, idiots, lunatics and members of the militia during service and after five years of service. Town boards may exempt the poor and infirm. No other poll tax.

GEORGIA—The state imposes a poll tax of $1.00 upon every person between the ages of twenty-one and sixty years. The blind and persons not owning $500 worth of property are exempt. Municipalities are prohibited from assessing poll taxes.

MARYLAND imposes no poll tax.

The foregoing are examples of the poll tax laws of states representing the different sections of the country. It will be noticed that none allows so large a poll tax as may be assessed in this State for state, county, town and highway purposes, and that, unlike Maine, the amount of the tax in nearly every state is a fixed definite sum. With a view to ascertain the judgment of experienced town officers, as to any desirable change in our poll tax law, we addressed inquiries to the assessors of all the cities and principal towns in the State, asking suggestions. We received replies from 120 boards. In these towns and cities a little more than seven per cent of the poll taxes are lost and abated. But the loss is mainly in the cities. Only nine cities reported, and in these the loss was from seven to fifty per cent, the average being twenty per cent. About half the towns assess a tax of $3.00 and the rest from $1.00 to $2.50. The largest percentage of losses are in the towns assessing the highest tax. The opinions of the assessors are varied and it is pretty difficult to get a definite result from them taken together, but they pretty well represent the condition of the public mind upon the general subject of taxation. Following are some of the suggestions :

Eight say, "The maximum tax should be $2.00."

Thirteen say, "Make the tax uniform throughout the state."

Nine say, "Make the payment of a poll tax a qualification to vote."

Six say, "Exempt all over 70 years old."

Five say, "Exempt all over 60 years old."

Three say, "Exempt all over 50 years old."

Some say, "The tax should not be over $1.00."

Others, "Let five dollars be the maximum."

Others, "Three dollars is little enough."

Others, "The law is all right as it is."

We have decided to recommend a change, not so much to put the poll tax provision of the law in harmony with the opinions expressed in these returns as to make it more in keeping with the laws of our sister states, and have taken away the discretion of towns and fixed it at two dollars for general purposes and not exceeding two dollars for highway purposes, making the age limits twenty-one and seventy years; other exemptions remaining as at present.

TAXATION OF DOGS.

As the system of taxation in nearly every state in this country includes provisions more or less elaborate for the taxation of dogs, and the disposal of the funds arising from such taxation, your Commissioners believed it to be their duty to examine the various methods adopted and recommend whatever, in their judgment, would improve our law upon this subject. Whether the dog is to be considered a domestic animal, as so eloquently and powerfully maintained by Chief Justice Appleton, dissenting in the celebrated dog case recorded in Vol. 75 Maine Reports, or to belong to the class of animals *ferae naturae* as the majority of the court there decided, all states have found it necessary, for the protection of sheep at least, to enact special laws to that end. While it may be true, as Judge Appleton asserts in the language of Cuvier, that barbarous nations owe much of their civilization above the brute to the possession of a dog, it is still true that many a sheep raiser owes much of his yearly losses to his neighbor's possession of a dog.

There are dogs and dogs. There always will be as broad a distinction in their natures as in their breeds, and the worst sheep killer among them may still be the "friend and companion of his master" and, as presumed by the common law, a tame animal "in the home, under the roof and by the fireside." The person who can afford the indulgence of such a friend and companion as a dog ought not to complain at any slight tax that may be imposed for the protection of property on which a tax is levied against the possible, or rather the probable, ravages of the canine race. As it is impossible to draw the line between those dogs that may be trusted and those that may not be, the tax must of necessity be general—a sort of mutual insurance against the sudden relapse of any of their number into his savage state and committing damage. The numerous instances of such damage, the yearly slaughter of sheep by dogs, to the discouragement in many sections of sheep husbandry, would seem to demand a better regulation than we have as to the taxation of dogs and a method of appropriating the proceeds of the tax to making good, as far as possible, such damages. The law, as it now is, effects but little. It is left discretionary with towns to impose the tax. In cities where the non-owners of dogs are more numerous than the owners of them, and where there are few sheep within reach of dogs, they are generally taxed, while in the farming towns they escape taxation, if the dog owners are more numerous or influential than the sheep owners. In the words of a farmer, "the dog ought not to be allowed to vote on this question." In fact, Maine is about the only State that leaves the matter open for the dog's influence. In the following states the legislatures have fixed the tax and provided for the disposal of the money arising from it:

	TAX.		How Appropriated.
	Male Dog.	Female Dog.	
Massachusetts,	$2 00	$5 00	
Connecticut...	1 15	6 15	For damages to sheep by dogs.
N. Hampshire,	1 00	2 00	For dam'ges to domestic animals by dogs.
Vermont......	$1 if paid April 1; $2 if paid by May 15.	Same	For general purposes.
New York	{ First dog $1; additional dog, $2.	{ $3.00. Each additional $5.00. }	} For gen'l purposes.
Maryland	$1.00	$2.00	For general purposes. But one male dog for each house is exempt.
Pennsylvania,	{ 25 cents first dog; second dog, $1; each additional, $2.	} Same	{ For dam'ges to sh'p by dogs.
Nevada........	$1.00	$1.00	For general uses.
Ohio..........	Valu'd and tax'd like other prop'ty		
Iowa..........	$0 50	$1 00	For dam'ges to domestic animals.
Illinois	1 00	1 00	For damages to sheep by dogs.
Michigan	1 00	3 00	For damages to sheep by dogs.
Wisconsin.....	2 00	3 00	Goes into the school fund.
No. Carolina...	1 00	1 00	Goes into the school fund.
Rhode Island..	1 15	5 15	For damages to sheep by dogs.
Virginia	First dog $1; each additional, $1.50.	Same	
West Virginia,	$ .50	$1.00	For damages to sheep by dogs.
New Jersey ..	{ First dog $1; each additional. $1.50.	} Same	{ Towns may tax $5 additional to the tax provided by law. Proceeds go to pay damages to sheep by dogs.

Indiana leaves it to the towns to vote to tax or not, but if they tax, the proceeds go to pay damages done to sheep by dogs. Georgia allows a dog tax to be imposed by constitutional provision, but we do not find any law among their statutes taxing them. The average amount of the tax upon each dog in the eighteen states named is $1.90. We recom-

mend a license tax, certain and uniform, of $1.00 on male
dogs over four months old and $2.00 on females over that
age; the proceeds to be applied, under suitable provisions to
prevent fraudulent claims, to pay for damages done by dogs
to sheep.

TAXATION OF MORTGAGES.

We have given considerable study to the vexed subject of
the taxation of mortgages. To tax or not to tax them is a
many sided question and most difficult of satisfactory solution. It involves the whole theory and practice of general
property taxation. The injustice of taxing a mortgage is
that it results in double taxation. If the real property mortgaged is taxed and the debt secured by it is taxed also, under
our system, the mortgagor is compelled, often, to pay a
double tax because the lender of the money, the mortgagee,
may and usually will make his contract to cover the tax he
may be obliged to pay on the mortgage indebtedness, and the
mortgaged property is taxable to the mortgagor. This liability to double taxation extends to many cases where no money
passes and the mortgaged property is the only property
involved. A has a piece of land worth $1,000; B has noth-
ing, but wishing to buy A's land, A conveys it to him, and
receives B's note for $1,000 secured by a mortgage of the
land. Under our system, the land is taxable to B and the
mortgage note to A, thus taxing $2,000 in value where but
$1,000 exists.

To give another similar illustration: A owns a farm worth
$2,000. B has $500 in money. Both are taxed in the aggregate $2,500. That is all the property they possess. B buys
A's farm and pays him the $500 in part payment and a promis-
sory note, secured by mortgage of the farm, for $2,500. No
new property has been created, yet our present system would
tax B for the land he has purchased $3,000 and A for the
debt B owes him $2,500, making $5,500 of taxable property.
Under such a system, the larger the amount of debts and

mortgages, the richer the community. "To tax both property and credits, both lender and borrower, is plainly incor-
rect in principle and inequitable in practice," says *Amasa
Walker*, author of *"Science of Wealth,"* and the foregoing
illustrations of frequent instances show the truth of the
criticism.

On the other hand, if mortgages are not taxed, the money
lender escapes taxation for the money he has loaned on mortgages altogether. How to adjust the tax so that exact justice
may be done to both borrower and lender and to prevent the
falling of all the taxes upon the borrower is the problem
challenging solution, and one which must remain without
absolute settlement until law shall usurp the power to make
contracts between borrower and lender,* or until all taxation
shall be removed from intangible property and choses in
action. It is not alone the relation of mortgagor and mortgagee that produces the injustice of double taxation. It
inheres in the whole system of taxing debts and securities
and property for which the possessor is indebted. It touches
the interests of all who do business, is peculiar to no class,
and is a grievance as old as taxation itself. In the earlier
days of our statehood, it was little felt, but in the multiform
methods of doing business at the present day, it is oftener
felt, and the evasions, subterfuges and frauds practiced to
avoid taxes upon credits and securities, are the chief cause of
the effort everywhere made to find a better system. It is a
most significant fact, and one which speaks forcibly of the
impracticability of statutory relief from double taxation in
case of mortgages that there has been so little accomplished
in any state to remedy it. In many states, as in our own,

*Note—Pennsylvania, by an act passed at the last session of its legislature, has attempted
to control the contracts between lenders and borrowers. Section 18 of "An Act to Provide
Revenue," enacts :
   "That from and after the passage of this act it shall be unlawful for any person or persons,
co-partnership, unincorporated association, limited partnership, joint stock association or corporation whatsoever, in loaning money at interest to any person or persons, whether such
loans be secured by bond and mortgage, or otherwise, to require the person or persons bor-
rowing the same to pay the tax imposed thereon by the first section of this act; and in all cases
where such tax shall have been paid by the borrorer or borrowers, the same shall be deemed
and considered usury, and be subject to the laws governing the same."

the tax payer is allowed to offset against debts due him an equal amount of his indebtedness, and in a few states he is allowed to offset his indebtedness against his valuation generally. In Massachusetts and Maryland, the legislatures have undertaken to deal with the subject of mortgage taxation, and in the latter state mortgages are not taxed. In Massachusetts, the mortgagee is taxed as joint owner with the mortgagor in the land mortgaged to the extent of his interest. This method was adopted under a statute enacted in 1881 and has proved reasonably satisfactory in practice.* The mortgage is taxed to the mortgagee as real estate to the

---

*NOTE.—This method is very highly extolled by the special committee on taxation of the Boston Executive Business Association in a report to the association last October. The association embodies the leading business associations of Boston, including the Chamber of Commerce, Merchants' Association, Master Builders' Association, Fruit and Produce Exchange and many others. On the subject of mortgage taxation, the committee say:

"In one thing to-day we are in advance of many states. Since 1883 real estate has been relieved from double taxation. It is regarded, as it should be, the property of the parties who have a deed of it, whether as mortgagee or having the fee; and the result is, as you all know, that the party who holds the equity, being the natural husband and care-taker of the property, by agreement with the mortgagee assumes the payment of taxes, and gets his money about the tax rate less.

    *   *.   *   *   *   *   *   *   *   *   *

"At length the merit of this reform gave it the victory, although it was nearly a seven years' war! And with what result to-day? We hardly know a person to whom it has not been a real gain, so universal and widespread its benefits.

"Let us enumerate some of them:—

"First. Real estate, relieved from double taxation, has become one of the most popular and profitable of investments, and year by year increases in value.

"Second. The rate of interest upon mortgages has fallen to so reasonable a figure that nobody complains; even the well-to-do business man can hardly afford not to have a mortgage upon his home, for present methods of doing business require so much capital that it is rare that he cannot make it earn more than four or four and a half per cent of a first-class mortgage, and the poor man, who used to be so victimized by the money lender, even on his small lower-class mortgage, need not pay over six per cent.

"Third. Massachusetts mortgages have become the best possible investment for trust funds, and the scanty income of the widow and orphan from this source is not required to be divided with the town or city in taxes.

Lastly. And this result please note. After the readjustment to the new order of things had taken place, there was no perceptible increase in the rate of taxation, and this reform, which puts millions into the pockets of the people, in the reduced rates of interest upon mortgages, and increased value of real estate, to all appearances costs the general tax-payer nothing."

To this Mr. Thomas Hill, the able chairman of the assessors of Boston, replied in an address to the association last January. Among other things he said:

"We all admit that the rate of interest on mortgages has fallen since the enactment of the law of 1881. Two years before that law went into effect the average rate of interest upon the mortgages of all parts of the State was six and twelve one-hundredths per cent. After seven years' operation the records show that the mortgages recorded in the first five months of 1889 were at an average rate of five and thirty one hundredths per cent, a difference of eighty-two one hundredths per cent. With the average tax of the State, as determined by its tax commissioner, at one and forty-seven one hundredths per cent, clearly the borrower has not received the whole advantage of the exemption, unless the rates of interest have been advancing during the last decade. That can hardly be, when within a week Boston has sold its three and one half per cents, liable to taxation, at a premium. We all know that interest has receded largely during the last eight years. All the concession that lenders of money upon mortgages have made to their borrowers they have been compelled to make by the laws of trade, not by those of the State. I am satisfied that were the laws that sustain the present exemption of mortgages repealed by the present Legislature, as mortgages fell due, the lenders would take the rate fixed by the money markets of the world, and pay their own taxes; and if they refused to do so, foreign capital would give borrowers all they required at that rate."

amount of the debt due him upon it, and the mortgagor is, to that extent, relieved from tax, as he is taxed only for so much of the value of the property mortgaged as is in excess of the debt ; thus making but one tax, in effect, upon the whole transaction ; the note being free of tax.   Thus the lender is taxed for the money loaned in the form of a tax on his interest in the mortgaged property and the borrower is relieved to that extent.   It is easy to see how, under this system, property escapes taxation, in theory at least, for if the lender retained his money and the borrower his land, both would be subject to full taxation.   But would the money be found for taxation ? It is also apparent that the lender's facilities for shifting the burden of the tax he is liable for to the shoulders of his debtor by extra charges, still remains.

On the whole, however, we conclude that the weight of the argument is in favor of some such method as Massachusetts has chosen, as compared with our own, and we have incorporated into our proposed law provisions of a like character. We are unable to devise any method that promises better results.

STREET RAILROADS.

The total amount of State taxes assessed upon the street railroad companies last year was $1,109.22.   The rate of taxation is so small as to be hardly worth the trouble of assessing and collecting. It would doubtless be a low estimate to set the total value of the roads yielding this amount of revenue to the State at $200,000.   Indeed, one road alone, the Portland Horse Railroad, was assessed $1,029.60 of the whole amount of taxes on street railroads, leaving but $78.62 for three others.   One road that cost about $20,000, whose stock is held at considerable in advance of par and which yields handsome dividends, pays a tax of $9.48.   Another road is assessed less than $1.00.

The rate of taxation of these roads is one-tenth of one per cent. of the gross receipts when they do not exceed $1,000 per

4

mile and one-tenth of one per cent. increase for each thousand or fractional part thereof additional. These roads are subject to local taxation for their buildings, lands and fixtures outside of their located right of way, which is but small, and to no other tax whatever. When it is considered that these street railroads are granted the valuable franchise of a right of way over the streets of villages and cities; with no land damages and rights of way to pay for, and often subjecting tax payers who have to pay to keep the streets in repair and safe for travel, to various annoyances, it would seem but just that they should be subject to local taxation; that the towns and cities whose streets they use should, at least, receive a tax from them. Why should the $50,000 more or less, which is invested in a business which runs cars through the streets of town be practically exempt from taxation, while the property of the manufacturer, the merchant, the farmer, who is obliged to make use of so much of the streets as the railroads leave for his use, is fully taxed?

It is urged by those who are interested in these enterprises that they are a public convenience and are as yet but tentative and in some cases do not pay. This may be said of about every business operation that is undertaken. The right of taxation cannot be made to depend entirely upon the success of a business enterprise. The merchant, the livery stable keeper, the hack and coach proprietor, the farmer, in fact all other classes of business-men have to bear their share of the public burdens, or are taxable for their possessions, whether successful or otherwise.

It has seemed to your Commissioners, therefore, that these corporations should not only be taxed more than they are now taxed, but that it should be a local tax, that the towns whose streets are yielded to their use, may receive such benefit or remuneration as a just tax on the value of the property of the corporation will give them. Our view is embodied in the law herewith presented. In cases where the street railroad extends into two or more towns, the act provides for a conference of the boards of assessors of the several towns whose roads are so used, to determine the value per mile of the entire road, track and, in case of electric roads, the poles and wires. So much of the value thus ascertained of the track, poles and wires as is located in each town, is taxed therein. The buildings, horses, cars and other property being taxable where located or usually kept on the first day of April. The corporation is relieved of all other taxation on its property, franchises and stock, excepting the small portion of the tax assessed on these roads towards the salaries and expenses of the railroad commissioners, and that the act provides shall be deducted from the local tax before payment to the town.

PUBLIC STREETS AND PRIVATE CORPORATIONS.

The subject of the use of the public streets by private corporations is becoming yearly of more importance in this country, by reason of the rapid increase of wires, poles and street railways. While the streets of Maine cities and villages have not yet, to a very cumbrous extent, been taken for the use of corporations, laws cannot be too early enacted to secure to towns some returns for the valuable rights and privileges which are secured through every charter, or incorporation under the general law, in the best public streets, for railways, telephones, telegraphs and electric companies. The city council of Boston has taken hold of the subject in that city. A committee has recently presented an able report containing much valuable data relating to the experience and practice of other cities in this and other countries in dealing with these corporations. We give herewith some extracts from this report as being applicable to Maine cities as well as to Boston, and because they contain valuable suggestions upon a subject which the legislature will be obliged before long to deal with. The committee say :

In almost every one of these cities, outside of our own, the corporations are required to make some direct return to the city for the privileges they enjoy in the public streets. This custom is so general that the claim that it would impose a burden upon corporations so serious as to impair their usefulness does not seem to have any force, and it is difficult to understand why such a result would be brought about in this city, or why the effect of such a system upon corporations should be any different in Boston than other cities.

"It will be observed, upon examining the communications, that the local telephone companies of Amsterdam pay to the city, annually, 21½ per cent. of their gross receipts, in St. Louis, five per cent. of gross receipts, and in Philadelphia, one dollar annually for each old pole and five dollars for each new pole, used for the support of wires. Street railway companies also pay large amounts for their locations. In Amsterdam they pay 5 per cent. of gross receipts annually; in Baltimore, 9 per cent. of gross receipts, with an additional tax on each car; in Newark, 2½ per cent. of capital stock; in Providence, a certain fixed sum; in St. Louis, a percentage of gross receipts on a sliding scale, while in New York state all street railway franchises are now sold at auction for the highest offer above a certain fixed percentage of gross receipts.

"While it seems to your committee most desirable that some return should be secured to the city from the corporations who hold and exercise these valuable and exclusive rights in the public streets, they appreciate the difficulty of introducing any system that will be applicable to all corporations alike, and will operate fairly in every case, without working an injustice to what are undoubtedly looked upon as vested rights. The method most generally adopted is to require the payment to the city of a percentage of the gross receipts. This method may work to advantage in many instances, but in the case of a street railway, telephone or electric light company, having its tracks or lines in different municipalities, it would be difficult to adjust the rate proportionately. In addition to this, it is not always possible to ascertain what a company's receipts actually are. The special tax upon each car of a street railway company, such as is levied in Baltimore, might tend to deter the company from furnishing adequate and proper accommodations for the community, especially if the fee, as in Baltimore, is greater for a new car than for an old one. The system is also open to objection as not being applicable to all corporations.

"As regards the auction system which has been adopted in New York, your committee are of the opinion that it would not operate satisfactorily in Boston under the present state of affairs, particularly in reference to granting street railway locations. If a street railway extension became necessary, and the proposed new location was offered at auction, a system of competition would at once be introduced in opposition to the present system of monopoly, which has received the sanction of the Legislature. A further objection to the system appears to be that it would tend to prevent a judicious and necessary railroad extension, on account of the reluctance which a corporation would evince to risk its rights upon the uncertainty of a public auction. Your committee are, however, favorably impressed with the method adopted in the city of Philadelphia, whereby a special annual fee is paid to the city for each pole belonging to the telegraph and telephone companies. The principle which underlies this system requires each corporation to pay a fixed sum for their special use of the public streets, and this sum is precisely proportionate to the extent of such use. The chief advantage of this system arises from the fact that it can be applied with equal fairness to each and every corporation enjoying the privileges granted them by the city. Thus, a street railway company might be required to pay the city a fixed sum for each mile of track located in the streets; telephone and other companies, operating lines of electric wires, to pay so much for each pole erected, and companies making use of pipes and conduits underground, a fixed sum per mile of pipe, etc.   *   *   *   *   *

"As it appears that the city at present has not the authority to secure a return from corporations to whom privileges are granted for use of the streets, it will be necessary to apply to the Legislature for further power, and the committee accordingly recommend the passage of the following order:

"ORDERED, That His Honor the Mayor be hereby requested to petition the General Court. at its next session, for the passage of an act authorizing cities and towns to prescribe terms and conditions for the use of their streets by private corporations."

EXEMPTIONS.

But little change is recommended in relation to exemptions from taxation. Ordinarily exemptions benefit most those who are best able to pay taxes, because they are usually the persons who possess to the fullest extent such property as is subject to exemption. An exemption of household furniture to the value of $300 to a family instead of $200 as in the present law, is recommended, because it is to be presumed that if the

proposed system is adopted and inventories are returned on
oath to the assessors, the wealthier householders will list considerable furniture value in excess of $300, whereas under the
present system it is very rare that any household furniture is
valued at all for taxation.   This will be a direct relief to people in poor or moderate circumstances.   It is very unusual
also, under our present law, that books—the family library—
is taxed.   Everybody will recognize the propriety of exempting a moderate value in books, to a family, although our
present law exempts none.   All are taxable, yet the practice
is not to tax them.   If, however, a person possesses a valuable
library, we see no reason why it should not be subject to
taxation as well as his musical instruments or carriages.
Large libraries and valuable books are usually owned by people able to pay taxes on them, while the small collection,
such as may be found or should be in the average family,
ought not to be taxed.   It is, therefore, proposed to exempt
family libraries to the value of $100.   In many states, the
exemptions of family libraries are from $100 to $500 in value.
The act also exempts the beds, bedding and kitchen utensils
requisite for each family.   Mules, horses and neat cattle less
than two years old are also exempt under the proposed act.
The present law makes them taxable if over six months old.

These extensions of exemptions, we believe to be proper
and in the interest of the farmers and other laborers of moderate means.

WHERE PERSONAL PROPERTY IS TAXABLE.

A good deal of property escapes taxation by reason of the
difficulty in understanding the present provision relating to
the taxation of personal property employed in trade, in building and the like.   It is claimed that much timber, logs, wood,
poles and the like, in transit from the forests, escapes taxation because having no place of taxation definitely fixed by
statute.   The present law provides that when any owner of real
estate notifies the assessors that any part of the wood, bark

and timber standing thereon has been sold by contract in writing and exhibits to them proper evidence, they shall assess such wood, bark and timber to the purchaser. The proposed law makes such property, while in transit or lodged upon the banks of streams and lakes, taxable to the owner in the town of his residence, hence must be included in his return to the assessors, if it is not assessed under the provision alluded to. Such property stored and piled in towns other than where the owner resides is taxable in the town where found. This may not appear just in all cases, yet it makes clear what is now obscure and will at least make such property pay its share of taxes somewhere.

STATE TAXATION.

It is believed by many that it may be possible to assess upon corporations an amount sufficient for State expenses, and thus the necessity for a property tax for State purposes be avoided. If this were possible within the limit of just taxation of corporations, it would, to a considerable extent, relieve the general tax burden of the people. But there are other questions, besides that of a slight decrease of taxation, to be considered in this connection. Would it be a wise and salutary thing to sever the financial ligament which now closely unites the State government with the town, and in fact with every individual? Would it be beneficial to the people at large to have the power and influence of corporations so immensely extended as they would be in case the State were dependent alone on them for its revenues?

It appears to us that such a policy would not be wise and that to resort to it would be to sacrifice an important principle, a paternal and unifying element of state government, at a very cheap price. There is little danger, however, that such a policy will be adopted in Maine for a long time, as it would not be possible, with any degree of justice, to levy all our State taxes upon corporations, especially if our system of distributions to towns for school and other purposes is to be continued.

The average amount annually derived by the State from property taxes, from 1880 to 1890, inclusive, was $853,-192.80. The assessments were as follows :

1880	5 mills per dollar,	$1,124,261 27
1881	4½ mills per dollar,	1,063,529 91
1882	4½ " "	1,063,529 91
1883	4 " "	945,430 92
1884	4 " "	945,430 92
1885	3¾ " "	886,399 18
1886	3¾ " "	886,399 8
1887	2¾ " "	649,487 11
1888	2¾ " "	649,487 11
1889	2¾ " "	649,487 11
1890	2¼ " "	531,697 17

This shows a very gratifying and steady reduction in the amount of property taxes for which the State annually calls on the people, and we are very confident that the levy will be further largely reduced if the legislature shall adopt the measures for additional sources of revenue herewith proposed. If, however, it shall be found that in the increase of revenues to the State and the decreasing demands of the treasury, the need of a property tax shall be reduced materially from the present rate of two and a quarter mills on the dollar, we trust the legislature in its wisdom will seek to reduce general taxation rather through the distribution system than by making the State independent of the towns and dependent wholly, or nearly so, on the corporations.

On this subject Chief Justice Marshall said : "The only security against the abuse of the taxing power is in the structure of the government itself. In imposing the tax the legislature acts upon its constituents. This is, in general, a sufficient security against erroneous and oppressive taxation. The people of a state, therefore, give to their government the right of taxing themselves and their property ; and as

the exigencies of government cannot be limited, they prescribe no limit to the exercise of this right, resting confidently on the influence of the legislature, and on the
influence of the constituents over the representatives to guard
them against abuse." Again he said: "The interest, wisdom, justice of the representative body and its relation with
its constituents, furnish the only security against unjust and
excessive taxation, as well as against unwise legislation generally." But how would it be in case all the expenditures of
the State, for which the legislature is called upon to provide,
is derived from corporations, and none from a general levy
upon the property of the people at large? Would not that
"*only security*" against unjust taxation and the abuse of the
taxing power, which the eminent jurist said depends on the
relations of the legislative body with its constituents, be, in
a great measure, wanting?

If it were not for the system of distribution, which is so
beneficial to a large number of towns, and the reliance of
the school system in many sections, the State might readily,
if it were desirable, soon obtain sufficient revenue for its
uses without taxing real estate, and even without new
sources. The taxes levied by the State on property this
year is $531,697.17. The amount returned to towns will be,
approximately, under the various laws requiring distribution,
$400,000, leaving less than $140,000 for purely State uses.
It should not be forgotten, when the question of State taxation is considered, that more than half the amount levied by
the State on property flows back again for the direct benefit
of the people.

The new direct sources of state revenues under the proposed law are: The taxation of collateral inheritances;
increase in railroad taxes by removing the three-and-a-quarter
per cent. limit; the taxation of sleeping car companies; the
taxation of telephonic instruments leased or royalty-paying;
the taxation of insurance and guaranty companies on gross
instead of net premiums; taxation of foreign and unlicensed
insurance companies; taxation of accumulations of savings

banks; taxation of trust and loan associations; taxation of corporate franchises; tax on enrollment and organizations of corporations, and taxes on private and special acts of legislation. The sums which may be reasonably expected from these sources, under a system administered by an efficient board of state assessors, in addition to the amount to be derived from present sources, will, we believe, be quite large. But it is from the increase of taxable property which will be brought to light by the system proposed, that we most confidently expect relief will be found for the general tax payer; in the new and imperative provisions which are intended to unmask the property of the dishonest, defeat the cunning of the evader, lessen the burden of the upright citizen and stimulate the fidelity of tax officers.

The average rate of taxation for all purposes throughout the State for 1889 was one and seventy-one hundredths per cent. on a valuation which in many towns was much below a "just value." We believe that, under the system proposed, the annual levy need not exceed an average of one per cent.

COLLATERAL INHERITANCES.

We have embraced in the system which we recommend a tax on collateral inheritances or property which goes by bequest or succession, or by deed or gift, to take effect after the death of the grantor, to persons not lineally related to the decedent. This tax is imposed in several states of this country and has long been a familiar source of revenue in several European countries. It has been strongly urged upon us by many leading citizens of the State, and we have made a careful examination of the laws imposing such taxes in the several states adopting them, their practical operation and the decisions of the courts touching their constitutionality. We have not thought it advisable to include direct inheritances although that, with a considerable exemption allowance, is strongly recommended by many. A tax upon collateral inheritances lays no burden upon common and natural suc-

cessions, such as from parent to child, or from child to parent. It reaches such property as through the permission and protection of the government, only, goes into the possession of persons or corporations who have had no hand in earning it. It is so given by statute and not by right, and it would seem, as remarked by the able special tax commission of Con-necticut, which included several professors of Yale Law School, in their report to the legislature of that state in 1887, that "the gift made by law may be properly taxed by law." It is an income without labor on the part of the receiver, property transferred by the assistance and protection of government from the dead to the living who has no proprietary rights in it. A tax of this kind is easily collectable which may also be urged as a reason for it. Questions of the con-stitutionality of special inheritance tax laws have arisen in every state where such laws have been enacted, but they have been sustained in every case excepting in New Hampshire, where a law taxing all estates, settled in probate courts of the state, one per cent. on their value and excepting only property passing by will or by law to the "husband or wife, children or grandchildren" of the deceased, was declared to be repug-nant to that provision in the New Hampshire Bill of Rights which limits the taxing power of the state to "proportional and reasonable assessments, rates and taxes upon all the inhabitants and residents within the state and upon the estates within the same." In the reasoning of the court in this decision, it seems to be conceded that if the uniformity of taxation required by the Constitution applied to property only, and not to inhabitants, the law would not have been unconstitu-tional, for in referring to decisions of the Court of Appeals of Maryland and of Virginia, where similar questions were raised and overruled, the New Hampshire Court say: "There is in that state (Virginia) no constitutional prohibition against taxing a civil right or privilege, or forbidding a discrimina-tion between lineal and collateral inheritances, because the requirement of uniformity applies to property only," and that,

while the Maryland Constitution provided "for a uniform
mode of taxation on property, it was not the purpose of the
framers of the Constitution to prohibit any other species of
taxation, but to leave to the legislature the power to impose
such other taxes as the necessities of the government might
require." In Virginia, the law was sustained as not imposing
a tax strictly upon property, but upon a civil right or privilege. As our state constitutional provision granting the
power of taxation, applies only to property and is more
nearly in accord with the provisions in the constitutions of
Virginia and Maryland, than it is with that of the New Hampshire Constitution, which requires taxes to be apportioned
equally among the inhabitants as well, we do not apprehend
that a collateral inheritance tax being of the nature of a tax
upon "a civil right or privilege," will be held to be objec-
tionable on the ground of unconstitutionality. The question
has been recently considered by the New York Court of
Appeals in the matter of McPherson, N. Y. Reports, 306,
where the court upheld the constitutionality of a law imposing "taxes upon gifts, legacies and collateral inheritances in
certain cases." The court there say; "It has been held in
several states where constitutional provisions required that
property taxes should be equal and uniform, that such provisions had reference only to general, annually recurring
taxes upon property generally, and not to special taxes upon
privileges or special or limited kinds of property."

The Connecticut legislature, at its last session, passed a
law taxing collateral inheritances, similar to the one embodied
in the act herewith submitted, after two years of reflection
upon the report of the tax commission which recommended
it. As to the propriety of such a tax, the Hon. Albert W.
Paine, in his report as Tax Commissioner, made to our legislature, session of 1874, said: "Where property is so situated as to pass to a new owner, who has had no agency in its
earning, it would seem to be only just and reasonable that a
small duty be paid to the state whose laws afford the passage."
We believe such will be the general opinion of the people.

The Comptroller of the state of New York in his last report to the legislature of that state, speaks of the inheritance tax law, which was passed there in 1885, as "a wise and just measure" and observes: "Under the law the immediate members of a person's family and those most equitably entitled to share in the property of a decedent are exempted from the tax prescribed; and only those gifts or shares of a decedent's property of the value of $500, or upwards, received by collateral relatives, who ordinarily have no equitable claim upon the bounty of the testator or intestate, are liable to the tax of five per cent. Such beneficiaries can well afford to pay a small tribute to the state, for if it were not for the wise and humane laws that the state has devised for their benefit and protection, they might not be entitled to receive the gifts upon which the small tax is imposed. Small estates pay very little or no tax. It is the large and wealthy estates that pay considerable amounts into the treasury for the benefit of the whole people."

A similar law has been upheld in North Carolina whose Constitution requires that all property shall be uniformly taxed and which limits the rate of state tax to two-thirds of one per cent. In the case of Pullen vs. The Commissioners of Wake County, (66 N. C. Reports, 361), the Court say: "Undoubtedly, if the tax in question must necessarily be regarded as a tax on property, the objection would be irresistible, since this property is not only taxed uniformly with other property, but is subjected to taxation as a legacy in addition. But we do not regard the tax in question as a tax on property, but rather as a tax imposed on the succession, on the right of the legatee to take under the will or of a collateral distribution in case of the intestacy. * * * Neither can it be held to be a tax on property merely because the amount of the tax is measured by the value of the property. The legislature may destroy the right of gift by will altogether—may it not regulate it and impose conditions on its exercise?"

Judge Cooley says, (On Taxation, p. 392), succession to an inheritance may be taxed as a privilege, notwithstanding the property of the estate is taxed and taxes are required by the constitution of the state to be uniform.

See also Hilliard on Law of Taxation, Ch. V., § 2.

Such a tax was strongly urged upon the legislature by Governor Plaisted in his address at the beginning of the session of 1881, in these words :

"As all property should bear its just and equal proportion of taxation, it would seem but reasonable that all legacies and inheritances should not go untaxed. The propriety of an inheritance tax distinguishing between lineal and collateral inheritance, is approved by the soundest political economists; nor can there be any doubt of the legal and moral right of the legislature to impose it   The conditions that make such a tax just and desirable, are that a large amount of personal property that passes by bequest—particularly government bonds—will escape taxation altogether, unless taxed when it comes to the light in its transfer from the dead to the living. Besides, it would seem but just and proper that this class of property should be made to contribute to the cost of maintaining courts of probate and of probate records, established and maintained for the sole benefit thereof. Then, again, the expenses attending the collection of this tax would be but trifling, and the burden of the tax would fall lightly upon those who pay it, because it would be deducted from what was never in their possession.   The state of Pennsylvania derives an annual income of over $300,000 from collateral inheritances and bequests, and in addition thereto a revenue of over $100,000 from a tax on wills, writs, deeds, etc."

The Maryland law taxes collateral inheritances, in excess of $500, two and a half per cent. which yields to the state about $45,000 a year.   The amount of this tax in 1887 was $45,594.

In a recent report of a Special Committee on taxation of the Boston Executive Business Association, the Committee thus forcibly recommend a tax of this kind :

One of the things, then, upon which your committee is agreed is to recommend a state tax, known in other states as the "Collateral Inheritance Tax."   Its name tells the story.

It does not reach the direct heirs, such as wife, children, parents, or even brothers and sisters, only collateral beneficiaries, persons and objects, who have no claim upon the estate, and get what they receive from the generosity of the donor, and the favoring circumstances of our law. What could be more reasonable than such tax in the final distribution of estates? Who should complain? Not the giver, for, if disagreeable to him, he may make his gifts during his lifetime. Not the receiver, for all should be to him an occasion of thankfulness. Would any of us object to such a tax for ourselves or for any charity with which we are identified? It is idle to reply that such a tax will be evaded by the testator. *The facts in other states do not show it*, and it would seem as if any reasonable man would, in disposing of any considerable portion of his estate to outside parties and interest, feel that a five per cent. tax thereon, paid to the state for public uses, might, indeed, be a very becoming and satisfactory way of meeting any particular default in taxation, or other source of obligation to the community and its laws.

This tax realized to the state of Pennsylvania—Collateral inheritance—

In 1888 over	$700,000
In New York in 1887	551,716
In New York in 1888	736,000
Estimated in 1889	1,000,000

While Maine bears no comparison with these large and wealthy states, yet we think a considerable revenue may be realized here from such a law if properly enforced. A very careful estimate made by the Connecticut Tax Commissioners of the probable annual income from the collateral inheritance tax law of three per cent., recommended for that state, based on inheritable property valued at $810,000,000, and an aggregate of collateral successions amounting to $1,780,516 was $54,415. If Maine possesses half as much, with a tax of two and a half per cent., there ought to be realized at least $20,000.

CORPORATE FRANCHISE AND ORGANIZATION TAXES.

There is no state, we believe, whose laws afford greater facilities for the organization of corporations, than do ours. By general law, in this State, three or more persons may form a corporation to carry on any lawful business with capital stock to the amount of two million dollars—excepting only banking, insurance, deposit, telegraph and telephone companies. No scheme is so visionary, provided its purpose is ostensibly "lawful business," that it may not become vested, by virtue of our laws, with organized powers and, in a sense, supported and indorsed thereby. It is only necessary to organize, fix the amount of capital stock which the company may sell, record the certificate of organization and receive the approval of the attorney general. No money is required to be paid in. The shares of stock constitute the basis of business and the merchandise in which the corporation is to deal. The state has, therefore, become the favorite organizing ground of corporations by speculators from other states, and it is not uncommon that at least a dozen of them, representing millions of stock in the aggregate, are born in a day. For the year ended December 31, 1889, three hundred and seventy-five corporations, aggregating more than one hundred and thirty-one million dollars of authorized capital, were organized under the general law in this State. The present year has been still more prolific of corporations, as, up to the first day of July last, two hundred and thirty corporations had been formed for "lawful business" since the first of the preceding January, with capital stock aggregating *more than eighty-three million dollars!* the month of June alone producing corporations with capital amounting to $20,608,000! The total number now in existence it is impossible to ascertain with accuracy, as the demise of many is unheralded and unrecorded; but more than 4,000 stand upon the records of the Secretary of State, as still possessing power for good or evil.

While our laws afford such unusual facilities for the inception of such corporation, they are singularly deficient in provisions for deriving any adequate revenue from them. Corporations formed for manufacturing and mining, for banking, for transportation, telegraph and telephone business, in fact all legitimate corporations which engage in business resulting in public welfare and owning property are subject to taxation. Such corporations generally consist of citizens of the state, but often of citizens of other states who seek investments here. The corporations which are not taxed are the hundreds formed for purely speculative purposes and may or may not have a legitimate basis of operation, or a place of business in this state other than nominal. Other states derive large revenues from such corporations, annually, besides a large amount from organization or enrolment fees. In New Hampshire a tax of $1.00 on each $1,000 of capital is imposed for bank charters, and $25 for each supplemental act. Savings banks, railroad and insurance charters pay 50 cents on each $1,000 of capital and all other corporations have to pay $50 each for charters. In Rhode Island the tax is $100 for charter and one-tenth of one per cent. of capital in excess of $100,000. In New York, all corporations, excepting a few which are otherwise taxed, are assessed one and a half mills on a dollar of entire capital annually, and if they pay dividends in excess of six per cent. they must pay one-fourth of one mill on every dollar of capital stock for each one per cent. of dividend in excess of six. This tax is for state purposes and in addition to local taxes. In Pennsylvania from $400 to $1,000 is levied on corporations by the state for charters, according to the amount of their capital stock. If the charter is to run more than twenty years the tax is doubled. Corporations are also taxed three mills on a dollar of value of capital stock. In New Jersey, an annual tax of one-tenth of one per cent. of the entire capital of corporations at par is required, and the result is enormous. Last year the state realized from 1,380 corporations $266,355.16 through this

5

one mill tax on capital, and in addition to the $1,405,613 received from railroad and other business corporations. It is unnecessary to cite the laws of the several states upon this subject. The above are enough to show precedents for taxing the capital stock at par of corporations and for charters or organizations.

That this is a constitutional mode of taxation is fully decided in the recent case of Home Insurance Company *vs.* New York, 134 U. S., 594. It is a tax on the corporate franchise, the right or privilege given to persons, by the state, of being a corporation. "This right or privilege to be a corporation," say the court in the above named case, "is one generally deemed of value to the corporators, or it would not be sought in such numbers as at present. It is a right or privilege by which several individuals may unite themselves under a common name and act as a single person, with a succession of members without dissolution or suspension of business, and with a limited individual liability. * * It (the state) may require, as a condition of the grant of the franchise, and also of its continued exercise, that the corporation pay a specific sum to the state each year or month, or a specific portion of its gross receipts, or of the profits of its business, or a sum to be ascertained in any convenient mode it may prescribe. * * * No constitutional objection lies in the way of a legislative body prescribing any mode of measurement to determine the amount it will exact for the privilege it bestows." In *California* vs. *Pacific Railroad Company* 127 U. S. 1, the court say: "The taxation of a corporate franchise * * * may be arbitrarily laid without any valuation put upon the franchises."

We have included in our bill provisions to cover both forms of taxation and with the confident belief that if the law does not result in a material increase of revenue to the State, it will at least have the effect to reduce the number of mushroom and noxious ventures which our general corporation laws encourage.

TAX ON PRIVATE AND SPECIAL ACTS OF LEGISLATURE.

Many states impose taxes or fees for private and special acts of legislation. There is much propriety in this. While it is a part of the duty of the legislature to enact certain laws for the benefit of private parties, yet its principal function is to enact general laws for the people. It has come to pass, however, in the multiplying conditions of business and the peculiar circumstances of communities that a very large portion of the time of the legislature is spent in investigating the propriety of special legislation or in the passage, or attempted passage of private bills. This consumption of time in special legislation narrows the time that can be devoted to the public business and causes much expense to the State for printing and in various other ways. It is very proper, therefore, that parties who are to be benefited by such legislation at the expense of the public, should contribute something to the State revenues.

The proposed bill imposes a tax of fifty dollars upon such special acts of legislation as are apt to consume most time and which often confer valuable franchises, and upon other private acts the sum of ten dollars.

ELECTRIC LIGHT, GAS AND WATER COMPANIES.

We have not included electric light and power, gas and water companies in the act herewith as subjects of special taxation. The bonds and stock which represents the value of such plants are taxable and, with such information as we have been able to get, we have not thought it necessary that further taxes should be required of them.

There may, however, be cases where such companies are yielding large dividends, where the bonds issued by them, if any, are beyond the reach of the assessors, and where the stock does not represent the value of the plant. Such a condition might make a tax on gross receipts, as in case of express companies, or a tax on the property of the company,

as in case of telegraph and telephone companies, advisable.
We leave it, however, for further investigation by the legislature to make such provision as may hereafter be expedient.

TAXATION OF INSURANCE COMPANIES.

Here again Maine is behind her sister states. Our present
law exacts taxes only on the net receipts of foreign insurance
companies, and, until 1885 did not tax domestic life insurance companies at all on premiums ; and since that date only
on net receipts. Of the forty states, including Dakota, whose
laws we have examined, only seven tax the net instead of gross
receipts, but in every such instance the tax applies to all
classes of insurance and domestic as well as foreign, while
in Maine the tax until 1885 was upon foreign insurance only.
In several states an annual license fee is charged in lieu of
all taxation against foreign companies doing business in those
states, of from $100 as in Nevada to $1,000 as in Virginia.
In fifteen states a tax is levied upon gross receipts, and, in
most of them, in addition to annual license fees. A table in
the appendix gives other details relating to insurance taxes
throughout the country.

We have made the taxes uniform in the bill submitted, two
per cent. on the gross receipts, allowing deductions for returned, unearned, premiums only, and have retained the provision authorizing retaliatory taxation. The present law
taxes the surplus funds of domestic life insurance companies
one-half of one per cent. We have made the tax in our bill
three-fourths of one per cent. the same as in case of savings
banks, and believe that will not be thought an unreasonable
tax for such protection as our laws and government afford to
property.

There is a class of insurance companies whose situs is beyond this State, but doing a large and increasing business in
this State without any license or lawful authority whatever
and paying no taxes or fees to the State. We have undertaken to incorporate provisions in our bill to prevent this

injustice to companies which pay for a license to do a legitimate business here and pay taxes on that business. These companies are known as mills mutual or factory companies and, according to the last annual report of the Insurance Commissioner, the risks written by the nineteen companies of this kind, all located out of the State, amounted in 1889 to $539,964,635, on which the premiums were $4,937,741. The losses incurred were $1,368,224 and the return dividends, $3,150,890, leaving for expenses, $418,627. The Commissioner says:

"It is evident that the business is a profitable one, and there is no good reason why it should not bear its just proportion of the burden of taxation. Licensed companies pay fees and taxes and are obliged to come into competition with these companies that pay neither. Other mutual companies pursuing like methods write upon protected property other than factories and the business all escapes taxation."

In Pennsylvania, recently, a bill passed the legislature granting to persons, companies and corporations permission to insure in these factory mutual companies. Governor Beaver vetoed the bill as being repugnant to that clause of the state Constitution which forbids the granting of exclusive privileges, all other insurance companies being subject to taxation by the state. The Supreme Court of the state has sustained the veto and declared the law permitting such insurance unconstitutional. We have no law permitting such insurance by our citizens in towns, yet much business is done by citizens of this state with these companies which have no agents nor office in this state, but operate through "inspectors." They thus keep beyond the reach of our law taxing insurance companies, claiming that the insurance is all effected at the home office.

"The method of reaching this business in Maine, inasmuch as it is written at the home office, is the problem necessary to be solved," says the Insurance Commissioner, with whose assistance we have incorporated provisions designed to solve the problem.

The bill seeks to reach the business of these concerns in this State through the inspectors who are made subject to the same license fees as other foreign insurance companies doing business here, and are required to give bond for guaranty of the payment of the tax on premiums received by the companies. Persons are subject to fine or imprisonment for doing any business for such companies as inspectors in the State, without first complying with the provisions of the bill as to bond and license.

The annual fees of insurance agents in Maine are but one dollar under the present law. In but four other states are they so small; in twenty-three states they are from two dollars to fifty per annum; in fifteen states the fee is two dollars; in four, five dollars; in one, six; and in one—South Carolina—fifty dollars per year. We recommend that the fee be increased to two dollars per year, and submit herewith a bill to amend section seventy-three of chapter forty-nine of the Revised Statutes, in accordance with this recommendation.

RAILROADS.

Our system of railroad taxation is the outgrowth of much legislation and practical experience. Whether the rate of taxation is as high as it ought to be is a question about which there may be honest difference of opinion. The railroads receive valuable rights and franchises from the people and in return confer great benefits upon the State in the extension and development of business. The railroad lines are the paths of progress in a hundred ways, and it is the policy of all the states to extend to them all reasonable encouragement. When they become rich and powerful they should be made to bear, like other successful business ventures, their fair share of the public burdens. The rate of taxes levied upon a railroad in the earlier days of its operations, may not be sufficient in subsequent years. The rate as applied to one corporation may be excessive as applied to another. The system of taxing the gross receipts is, doubtless, as fair a way as any, for by that method the levy is graduated to the amount of business the road is doing.

Since 1881, railroad companies in this State have been subject to taxation as follows:

First: All buildings of the corporation, and its lands and fixtures outside of the located right of way, are subject to local taxation by the towns in which they are located. Second: They are subject to an excise tax, payable to the State, and by the State returned to certain towns, to the amount of one per cent. on the value of stock of such railroad companies, owned in those towns. The amount of such excise tax is found by dividing the gross amount of transportation receipts by the number of miles of railroad operated, to ascertain the average gross receipts per mile. When such average per mile does not exceed $2,250, the tax is one quarter of one per cent.; not exceeding $3,000 per mile, one-half of one per cent., and so on, increasing the rate one-quarter of one per cent. for each additional $750 per mile or fractional part thereof, *provided*, that the rate shall in no event exceed three and a quarter per cent. Third: By Act of 1889, Chap. 313, Sect. 4, railroads are made subject to a special tax to meet the salaries and expenses of the board of railroad commissioners. This system, which the legislature in its wisdom has so recently adopted, we do not deem it expedient to change, especially as it is in harmony with the more recent systems adopted in several of the states. We are of opinion, however, that the time has arrived when the limitation to three and one-quarter per cent., beyond which the gross receipts per mile cannot be taxed under the present law, may be removed, and in the bill herewith reported that restriction will not be found.

For the purpose of comparison, and to aid in judging whether our laws are keeping step with those of other states in the matter of railroad taxation, we append brief abstracts of the laws of many other states on that subject.

MASSACHUSETTS—Tax upon franchise as in case of all other corporations and collected by the state. The valuation is found by local assessors as follows : The market value of the shares is ascertained and the aggregate value computed. From this is deducted the assessed value of real estate locally taxed. Upon the balance the tax is assessed at the average rate of all the towns in the state. The tax is divided among the towns in which shareholders reside according to the number of shares owned therein, being offset against said town's portion of state tax. Taxes on non-resident holders of stock are retained by the state. When railroads run into other states the assessment is made in proportion to the length of the road in the state compared with its entire length.

VERMONT—Until 1882, railroads were valued and assessed by a board of state appraisers at a fixed sum per mile, similar to the western method. In 1882, the mode was entirely changed and the system of taxation on gross earnings per mile of road in the state, as in Maine, was adopted,—only the tax is much larger than in this state, being two per cent. on the first $2,000 per mile, and on total earnings if less than that sum; three per cent. on the first $1,000 in excess of $2,000 per mile; four per cent. on the first $1,000 above $3,000 per mile and on all earnings in excess of $4,000 per mile five per cent.

Railroads taxed like other property on the grand list at a uniform valuation per mile of road-bed, assessed by three state appraisers, the total number of miles in each town, of such road-bed, is taxed by the town at such average valuation. Stations and other buildings are taxed separately in towns where located.

CONNECTICUT—Railroads pay the state a tax of one per cent. on the valuation of their stock, one per cent. on par value of their bonded and floating debts not held as a sinking fund, unless the same is worth less than par, then on true value, deducting also the value of any real estate owned by the company. Company shall pay the tax, and have lien on the stock for payment. When only part of the railroad lies within the state, then to be taxed by the state on its capital stock, &c., proportionately. Railroad not to be taxed otherwise, except on its real estate.

NEW HAMPSHIRE—Railroads are taxed by the state for the value of their road including rolling stock and equipments within the state. The value to be ascertained by state board of equalization, for which purpose said board appoints a time for hearing in relation to the matter. If the representatives of the railroad appear and give information at such hearing said board values such railroad as aforesaid, and assesses on such valuation a tax at the average rate of taxation throughout the state; otherwise to be doomed two per cent. on its entire authorized capital and debt. The above valuation and tax includes all buildings. Railroads are exempt from taxation for ten years after their construction.

The tax collected of railroads by the state as aforesaid is apportioned and credited as follows: One-quarter among the towns through which the road runs in proportion to the amount of the capital stock expended therein for buildings and right of way. To each town in the state in which stock is owned, such proportion of the residue of the tax as the number of shares owned in such town bears to the total number of shares in such corporation. The remainder of such tax to be retained by the state.

NEW YORK—Taxes are imposed on their real and personal property, in towns through which the roads run, for local purposes. In addition to such taxes, every railroad, express, canal, steamboat, ferry, elevated railway or other transportation company, foreign or domestic, doing business within the state, pays the state for state purposes a tax of one-half of one per cent. on gross receipts within the state. Real estate of such corporations is subject to local taxation but capital stock is exempt from other state taxation.

KANSAS—The value per mile of railroad beds are ascertained annually by state board of railroad assessors. Said board values the entire road within the state, including the value of the franchise, road-bed, right of way, track, rolling stock, telegraph wires and instruments. material on hand and supplies, tools and other property used in operating such road, together with all money and credits on hand.   Then ascertains the total number of miles of such road within the state and the value per mile, and the number of miles in each town through which such road runs.   On this valuation the local tax is based at its rate for general taxation.

ILLINOIS—Railroad property, for purposes of taxation, is classified under four separate heads and taxed accordingly.

The *railroad track* is assessed in each county, town and city in proportion that the length of road therein bears to the whole length of the line in the state.   Side and second tracks, stations, machine shops, &c., assessed by the towns in which they are located.

The *rolling stock* is taxed by the counties, towns and cities in the proportion that the whole length of line in such county, &c., bears to the whole length of road in the state.

The *personality*, viz., tools, materials for repairs and all other personal property, except rolling stock, is taxed in the county, city or town in which it may be on the first of May.

The *capital stock* of railroads is valued by the state board of equalization in the aggregate and distributed proportionately to the several counties, and by the counties to the several towns entitled to a proportionate value, in the same manner that the value of a "railroad track" is distributed, and such stock at such valuation is taxed the same as other property in such towns.

INDIANA—The method of taxing railroads in this state is similar to that adopted in Illinois.

PENNSYLVANIA — Railroads, steamboats, canal and other corporations over whose works freight is carried, are obliged to make quarterly return stating the number of tons of freight transported and to pay the state a tax at the following rates per ton: On raw products of quarries, mines and clay beds two cents a ton; on hewn timber, products of forest, agricultural products unwrought three cents a ton; on all other articles five cents a ton. When the same freight is carried over different but continuous lines of transportation, but one tax shall be charged to be borne proportionately by such corporations.

In addition to the aforesaid taxes every railroad and other corporation liable to tonnage tax, is required to pay three-quarters of one per cent. tax on gross receipts.

NOTE—By act of legislature of June, 1889, this mode was changed. The capital stock is now taxable at the rate of one-half mill upon the capital stock for each one per centum of dividend and eight mills on the dollar of gross receipts.

OHIO—Railroad property is taxed by towns at local rates in substantially the same manner as in Illinois, excepting that the valuation is fixed by a county equalizing board instead of state board.

WISCONSIN—(As amended by chapter 285, laws of 1889.) The track, right of way, depot grounds and buildings, machine shops, rolling stock, and all other property necessarily used in operating any railroad, belonging to any railroad company, including pontoon, or pile and pontoon railroads, are exempt from taxation for any purpose, except that the same are subject to assessments for local improvements in cities and villages, and all lands of any such railroad company, not adjoining the tracks of such company, are subject to all taxes. This does not apply to any railroad operated by horse, cable or electrical power.

IOWA—Railroads are taxed substantially as they are in Kansas.

VIRGINIA—The tax assessed by the state is thirty cents on every $100 of the assessed value of the road for government purposes, ten cents on $100 for free schools and a tax of one per cent. on the net income of the road.

MICHIGAN—Railroads, on or before the first day of July in each year, pay to the State Treasurer, on the statement of the Auditor General, an annual tax upon the gross receipts of the company, computed in the following manner, viz., upon all gross receipts not exceeding four thousand dollars in amount per mile of road actually and regularly operated for the conveyance of passengers and freight, two per cent. of such gross earnings; upon such gross receipts in excess of four thousand dollars per mile so operated, three per cent. thereof; which amount or tax shall be in lieu of all other taxes upon the property of such companies, except such real estate as is owned and can be conveyed by such corporation under the laws of the state, and not actually occupied in the exercise of its franchises, and not necessary or in use in the proper operation of its road; but such real estate so excepted is liable to .taxation in the same manner, and subject to the same conditions as to assessment for taxation, as is other real estate in the several townships within which the same may be situated.

MINNESOTA—Every railroad has the option of paying tax on gross earnings (to be in lieu of all other taxation) as follows: For the first three years, one per cent.; for next seven years, two per cent., and thereafter three per cent. of gross earnings. This is a state tax, and is a substitute for all other taxation, even including land granted to aid in construction.

KENTUCKY—The same rate of taxation for state purposes, which is levied on other real estate, is levied upon the value of the railroad, rolling stock and real estate of each company; and the same rate of taxation for the purposes of each city, town, county or tax-district, in which any portion of any railroad is located, which is levied on other real estate therein, is levied on the value of the real estate of railroads therein.

NEW JERSEY—State board of assessors value railroad property in the state, including road-bed, tracks, buildings, etc., and all tangible personal property, franchises, rolling stock, etc., deducting from the aggregate, mortgage debts (taxed to creditors). On this valuation a state tax of one-half of one per cent. is assessed, and the railroad is also subject to a local tax on all real estate, buildings and track not included in "Main Stem," assessed by the state board and distributed to the several towns where located, *pro rata*, not exceeding one per cent.

MARYLAND—The real and personal property of all railroads worked by steam, including bridges and tunnels in the value of the road-bed, but not at a higher rate than other portions of road-bed, is taxable in the several counties through which such railroads run, like other property therein situate for local purposes.

Said railroads are also required to pay the state a tax of one-half of one per cent. of gross receipts, within the state, to be in lieu of all other state taxation.

SAVINGS BANKS.

Very early in our investigation into the causes of complaint, we were strongly urged to recommend an increase of the tax upon savings banks. It was claimed by those who represented the interests of farmers that these banks were absorbing the money of the State, thus placing it beyond taxation, except the three-fourths of one per cent. for State purposes, and that it was their policy to discriminate against real estate security for loans, hence that they were of little or no practical benefit to the borrowers for purposes of accommodation. It was also charged that these banks were investing largely in the national bank and other taxable stocks of the State, and thus removing them from the reach of the assessor, as it is claimed by the managers of the savings banks that stocks purchased and held by them are not subject to local taxation. It is the policy of all the states, in which there are savings institutions to deal liberally with them in the matter of taxation. They are everywhere acknowledged to be of great benefit to the State and taxes are adjusted to favor them, but, by comparison, our law relating to taxation of savings banks will be found more liberal than that of some other states, or, at least, it is more liberally construed in practice.

In this State, savings banks and institutions for savings pay a State tax of three-fourths of one per cent. annually on the amount of deposits. Deposits are exempt from municipal taxation. The deposits are subject to deductions for the amount of United States bonds and (by act of 1887, chapter 64) shares of corporate stocks such as are by law of this State free from taxation to the stockholders and the value of real estate owned by said bank or institution. The statute does not include, specifically, trust and loan associations as being subject to this State tax, although they are institutions for savings and hence included in the spirit of the law. As we know no good reason why their deposits should not be taxed, we have included them in the proposed law. The trust companies of the State now represent about $2,500,000 ; more than $1,500,000 of which is in deposits and less than $800,000 in capital stock. We give below a synopsis of the savings bank tax laws of other states.

MASSACHUSETTS—A state tax of one-half of one per cent. is imposed on the amount of deposits in savings banks, deducting value of real estate owned and used by the bank and real estate mortgaged to secure loans. So much of this tax so paid as is on account of shares in banks, which are the absolute property of the savings bank and subject to local taxation, after the amount is determined by the Tax Commissioner, is deducted from the next tax payable.

VERMONT—Savings banks and trust companies are taxed one-half of one per cent. on amount of their deposits and accumulations, after deducting amount of real estate owned, and also amount of individual deposits in excess of $1,500 each, which excess is taxed in the town of depositor's residence.

NEW HAMPSHIRE—A corporation tax of $100 on each savings bank is provided. Real estate is subject to local taxes. On all deposits and accumulations, less the value of real estate locally taxed, a state tax of one per centum is imposed. The tax is distributed among towns in which depositors reside *pro rata*.

MARYLAND—The state tax on savings banks is one-quarter of one per cent. on total amount of deposits, not excepting assessed value of real estate subject to local taxation.

CONNECTICUT—A state tax of one-fourth of one per cent. on deposits exclusive of surplus, deducting $50,000 and amount invested in bonds of the state or of any town in the state in aid of any railroad, which bonds are exempt from taxation by state law; also deducting value of real estate owned by the bank.

RHODE ISLAND—Savings banks and trust companies are taxed for state purposes on total deposits and reserve profits. No deductions.

NEW YORK—Deposits in savings banks are not specifically taxed. But real estate and stocks owned by them are subject to taxation the same as other property.

PENNSYLVANIA—Savings banks are taxed one per cent. on the par value of their shares and exempt from all other taxation. They pay $100 for charter fee.

By a usage which we believe is without exception in this State, national bank stock owned by savings banks is not taxed locally. There is no direct provision of law under which such exemption can be claimed, nor is there any provision which, except by a forced implication, would take bank stock out of the list of taxable property, because owned by a savings bank. The statute, chapter 6, section 66, exempts all deposits from municipal taxation, but there is no express provision exempting stocks otherwise taxable. The law expressly exempts from taxation to the savings banks so much of their deposits as are represented by stocks which "are free from taxation to stockholders," and, under the familiar rule of law that the inclusion of one excludes the other, it would seem pretty clear that stocks which are not free from taxation to the stockholder are not free because held by a savings bank   Exemption from taxation can only be claimed by virtue of direct statute. An implication is not enough. A similar usage had grown up among the savings banks of Maryland. The law of that state declares that "no other tax" (than the state tax on deposits) "shall be laid on such bank, institution or corporation in respect to such deposits." The Maryland Tax Commissioner in his Annual Report to the General Assembly, last January, said : "A few such banks were of the opinion that this provision in the law worked an exemption from taxation of any investment they might choose to make, but when informed that exemption from taxation can only be made in express terms by law and cannot be inferred, they, with one exception, I believe, came to the conclusion that their former opinions were wrong. All of them, however, acquiesced in the decision as made. The only investments, the ownership of which could raise such a question, under the law, are the shares of stock of banks or other corporations of this state, upon which the taxes are required to be paid by such banks or other corporations. The taxes being thus required to be paid, the ownership of such shares by a savings bank or institution could not affect their taxation, unless the law should so unequivocally declare." The Commissioner then adds pointedly : "This would be a very unwise provision and is such an one as no prudent legislature would ever adopt." If, however, shares of stocks otherwise taxable to the holders are taxed to the savings banks when owned by them, by local authorities, and thus included in the general mass of personal property for general taxation, the special state tax should be remitted on so much of the deposits as is represented by such stock.

The savings banks claim also exemption from taxation of their accumulations. The "surplus" funds of the savings

banks of Maine, as appears by the last annual report of the
bank examiner, amounted to more than five and a half million
dollars, an increase of one million and a half since 1884, or
an average increase of $300,000 a year.

This large sum is not reached at all for taxation by State,
county or town. Was it the intention of the legislature that
it should pay no taxes? They have not so expressed themselves in any law. It is only by implication again that such
exemption can be claimed, and the implication, even, seems
to us somewhat strained. In New Hampshire and Vermont
the statutory provisions are explicit, and extend the tax to
"deposits and accumulations." It is the policy of the several states to foster within reasonable limits all institutions of
savings. They teach thrift and economy, materially add to
the prosperity of the community, and in a considerable
degree prevent want and distress. Maine has recognized the
great benefits of her savings banks in these respects, and the
people have learned to rely upon their conservative, wise and
reliable management as absolutely safe places for their earnings. Safety, indeed, is the first and main object of their
creation. Large dividends from such institutions are not for
the best interest of the State. The legislature has wisely
limited them to not exceeding five per cent. per annum. Several savings banks paid up to the limit last year, the average
for all the banks being four and a half per cent. With dividends above four per cent. per annum, capital is attracted
toward these banks, and, although the statutory limit for a
depositor is $2,000, there are many ways in which the law is
evaded. We think, therefore, that without crippling these
excellent institutions, or in the least impairing their soundness, the State tax should be extended to their accumulations. We make no recommendation as to the taxation of
stocks held by these banks as investments, incorporating in
our bill the present law, which gives sufficient authority. By
far the larger part of the investments of these banks and
associations, in the aggregate, are made out of the State.

6

They yield larger rates of interest than home investments. As
a measure for the encouragement of home loans and investments, and in some degree to equalize the difference in interest, the bill makes a difference of one-half of one per cent.
in favor of home investments; the tax on these is fixed at
one-half of one per cent., and on such amounts as are invested
in other states, it is one per cent. We believe this distinction will have a considerable tendency towards keeping these
deposits in the State and in circulation among our own people.
At the suggestion of the State Treasurer we have changed
the time for the semi-annual payment of savings banks taxes,
making it a week earlier.

Table No. 3, in the appendix, shows the aggregate deposits
in the savings banks from 1874 to 1889, with other statistics
relating to them. The record is a convincing one as to the
conservative management and prosperous condition of these
banks.

LOAN AND BUILDING ASSOCIATIONS.

This new form of co-operative institutions, which are fast
getting a foothold in this State, we have not included among
taxable corporations. There are now nineteen in practical
operation, as reported by the bank examiner, and they represent in the aggregate loans to the amount of over $350,000.
Some are yielding a fair dividend to the shareholders, we
are informed, and the institution is regarded as very helpful
to those who, through its agency and help, secure homes.
We do not think the time has yet arrived when they should
be taxed, although in some states they are assessed. In New
Hampshire a tax of one per cent. is levied upon the whole
amount paid upon the stock or shares of these associations
which are in force. It should be remembered that the osten-
sible object is to assist shareholders to build residences. In
so far as this is done, they add materially to the taxable
property of the State.

LAND SALES FOR TAXES.

We have incorporated the machinery of the old law, so far as practicable, relating to the collection of taxes, but have endeavored to reduce to a less complicated method the provisions for enforcing collection of taxes on lands. The tribulations of tax officials in attempting to secure delinquent taxes on lands have become notorious and it has long been an axiom among lawyers that a tax title is *prima facie* void. The troubles arising under proceedings to sell lands to secure the taxes thereon and the dubious character of the title thus conferred to the purchaser, are by no means peculiar to Maine. No legislature of any state, so far as we have ascertained, has been wise enough to devise a method of procedure in such cases, which is at once clear, explicit and just and which does not somewhere conflict with settled rules of law touching the construction of statutes which aim by processes *in invitum* to transfer titles to property. Nearly half of the tax laws of some states are devoted to regulations for this purpose, but, so far as we can see, the vexed questions of tax titles are as often before the courts of those states for decision as in states with more comprehensive laws to regulate tax sales. The main difficulty is that in such cases the law justly requires that the provisions of the statute in all particulars be strictly complied with. As collectors of taxes are often persons who are little accustomed to construing statutes, and sometimes quite illiterate, it is not strange that fatal errors should be committed by them in undertaking to follow a statute requiring such punctilious performance.

The difficulties are stated in a communication of Hon. Ephraim Flint of Dover, a lawyer of much experience in such cases, which has been published. He says : "In a large portion of our towns there are no persons of sufficient skill or capacity in the work of assessing and collecting taxes to do such work in conformity to all the statute requirements. This should not be regarded as any disparagement to such towns, as our tax laws, in many respects, are blind and intricate. Especi-

ally should such towns be exonerated from all discredit when
we consider that our legislature, the embodied wisdom of the
state, and some of our state treasurers have made fatal mistakes in the assessment and collection of state taxes;" as
appears by several cases which he cites from the Maine
Reports.   To illustrate the hardships which may result to
towns from the well understood defects inherent in these proceedings, Mr. Flint cites the instance of a town in Piscata-
quis county which has become involved in a debt of *more
than sixteen per cent. of its entire valuation* because, intimi-
dated by proprietors who deny the legality of the taxes and
proceedings of sale, "the town has year after year settled a
portion of the taxes at a ruinous discount, but in a majority
of cases has been unable to collect any amount."

Intelligence is the first requisite of an efficient collector of
taxes, and it can hardly be expected that a law of so much
importance and detail, and which assumes so much power as
to take the property of one individual and transfer it to
another without the consent, or possibly the knowledge, of
the owner, should be adapted to the comprehension of the
illiterate or the dullard.   Yet it would seem possible that its
provisions could be made sufficiently plain for that degree of
intelligence which is characteristic of the native population
in every town in this State.   The present law is unnecessa-
rily complicated and obscure.   It provides, without any sufficient reason, two methods of procedure in the collection of
delinquent taxes on lands.   One for the sale of lands of non-
resident and the other for those of resident owners, and
while a part of the requirements are materially different, a
part are essentially the same, leading to confusion.

The provisions of the present law relating to sales of lands
for non-payment of assessments thereon for roads in unincorporated places, make no distinction between lands of resident
and non-resident owners, in the proceedings, nor do we find
in other states such distinction made.   We have undertaken
to divest the law relating to all tax sales, of some of its
obscurities, and have obliterated the distinction between cases

of resident and non-resident proprietors, making the proceedings the same in all cases, taking care that due notice to the owner or his agent shall in all cases be given before sale, and ample opportunity for redemption and correction of mistakes. At the same time we recognize that the proprietors, whether resident or not, owe some duty to the state, to the tax laws and to the town in which their property is located.

In many cases of defective sales of land for taxes, it will be found that trouble arose from a defective description of the property taxed, in the original list. The list is the foundation of all subsequent proceedings. Each document in the process to enforce payment, wherein the land is designated, depend on the accuracy of its description. A defective description in the list runs through the warrant to collect, the notices, returns, records, certificates and deeds. These latter may be corrected or cured by amendment, but that will not cure the original difficulty. Unless the list description is correct, the officer has but a blind guide in advertising and selling the land. It is absolutely essential that the description in the list however much of labor it may entail upon the assessor, should be accurate enough to designate the land and notify its owner, beyond question, that it is assessed or in jeopardy of sale. The description is required to be of greater nicety even than in a deed of conveyance between man and man. There the owner is a party to the sale. The ambiguity in the description may be explained. But not so in tax sales. There the owner has nothing to do. The government is acting through its officers and in hostility to him. Nothing can be supplied by intendment.

In consolidating the provisions of the two methods, we have endeavored to preserve as much as possible of the essential details of the proceedings with which collectors may be supposed to be familiar, but have tried to include in one direct and consistent course all the details for notices, advertisements, sales, returns and records. The bill also provides a remedy by lien and its enforcement by suit. It was not a

task without difficulty, and we do not expect that the result
will be found in practice free from defects, but feel confident
that it will, at least, be found no more defective than the
present law.

REPEALING ACT.

We have thought it advisable to report a draft of a repealing act for the convenience of the legislature in case our
principal bill should be adopted in the form reported.   The
repealing act includes all the acts which we have consolidated
in the principal bill, passed since the last revision of the
statutes.   In every instance but one the provisions of the
acts passed since the revision, and included in the repealing
act, have been adopted as passed.   The exception is chapter
seventy-two of the Public Laws of 1887, which so amends
the law taxing express corporations, companies and persons
as to exempt from taxation an express business carried on by
individuals not incorporated.   As we are unable to see a
sufficient reason for such exemption we have not incorporated
it in the principal bill.   The propriety of the passage of this
repealing act or any portion of it will of course depend upon
the action of the legislature touching the principal bill, but
we have collated the various acts additional and amendatory
of chapter six in that form as a matter of convenience if any
repeal shall become necessary.

CONCLUSION.

The result of our labors is not, properly speaking, the
recommendation of a new system of taxation.   A new system
could hardly be framed without a change in the Constitution.
But many of the proposed provisions are new to our law and
radical.   We have acted on the belief that the people demand
something more than a little tinkering of the law here and
there by acts amendatory and additional.   That course has
been pursued until our tax laws are a patchwork of provisions
often confused and singularly inefficient as revenue laws.   We

believe that the legislature declared by the resolve under
which this Commission was appointed, that the time has
arrived when Maine should put itself in line with other pro-
gressive states in her methods of taxation. With this view
we have worked. Such changes as the times and circumstances demand cannot well be made by more patching of the
laws. In order to make the changes we conceive to be demanded and believe to be necessary, an entirely new draft of
chapter six of the Revised Statutes was required, as several of
the new provisions effect a large part of the chapter. We
have tried to make the law more systematic and direct, com-
bining in a more united scheme state and local taxation.
While the towns are left independent as heretofore, the plan
for listing and state supervision which we propose makes their
interest and that of the State and county identical, in revenue
matters, and erects a substantial barrier against undervalua-
tions by town assessors to cheat the revenues of the State and
shift the burdens to towns whose assessors are more conscientious in following the obligations of their oaths of office and
the explicit requirements of the Constitution. The board of
state assessors—the head of the system—by a general oversight, and by visiting all sections, by frequent state valuations,
is calculated to give a coherence, equality and unity to the tax
system which have heretofore been wholly wanting.

It is only after a great deal of discussion that we have ven-
tured to recommend some of the more important changes, and
we do not expect them to be adopted by the legislature without much consideration.

We fear, also that there may be found in the proposed bill,
defects of construction and arrangement and quite probably,
inconsistencies which the experienced eyes of legal gentle-
men in the legislature may discover, or which may be left for
practical tests or judicial examination to disclose; it would
be phenomenal indeed if many faults should not be found in
these respects. We ask that it may be charitably considered
that the time in which we have been obliged to complete the
comprehensive task committed to us has not been a long one

when it is remembered that your Commissioners were much of the time necessarily engrossed by the demands of private business. We feel very confident, however, that our propositions will grow in favor the more they are discussed and the reasons therefor are studied, and that whether they shall be approved by the legislature or not, our labors will prove of substantial value. Our aim has been to propose a law which, before everything else, will equalize the burden of taxes, and thus lessen the rate everywhere; decreasing the assessment of the just and conscientious citizen by increasing to its proper limit that of the tax dodger. That we have hit upon perfect measures to that end we do not claim, for duplicity and cunning defy the most rigorous statutes; but we have hope that our labors, if approved and the result embodied in the will of the people, will give them substantial relief. In such faith we respectfully submit our work, through the hands of your Excellency, to the Honorable Legislature.

OLIVER G. HALL,
SAMUEL J. ANDERSON,
JOHN L. CUTLER.

AN ACT TO PROVIDE FOR THE RAISING OF REVENUE BY TAXATION.

Poll Taxes.

SECT. 1. A poll tax of two dollars and no more for town, county and state purposes, except highway taxes separately assessed. shall be assessed upon every male person between the ages of twenty-one and seventy years, whether a citizen of the United States or an alien. in the place where he is an inhabitant on the first day of each April, unless exempted therefrom by this chapter. No person shall be considered an inhabitant of a place on account of residing there as a student in a literary institution. Not exceeding two dollars in one year may also be assessed on each taxable poll for highway taxes when separately assessed ; and the residue of such taxes shall be assessed on property acc rding to its value.

Property Taxes.

SECT. 2. All real property within the state, all personal property of inhabitants of the state, and all personal property hereinafter specified of persons not inhabitants of the state. is subject to taxation as hereinafter provided

SECT 3. Real property, for the purposes of taxation, except as provided in section six, includes all lands in the state and all buildings erected on or affixed to the same, and all townships and tracts of land, the fee of which has passed from the state since the year eighteen hundred and fifty, and all interest in timber upon public lands derived by permits granted by the

—land and interest in timber, taxable.

Commonwealth of Massachusetts ; interest and improvements in land, the fee of which is in the state ; and interest by contract or otherwise in land exempt from taxation.

R. R. buildings, &c., subject to municipal tax, as non-resident land.

SECT. 4. The buildings of every railroad corporation or association, whether within or without the located right of way, and its lands and fixtures outside of its located right of way, are subject to taxation by the cities and towns in which the same are situated, as other property is taxed therein, and shall be regarded as non-resident land.

Street Railroads.

Street railroad property subject to local taxation.

SECT. 5. The property of every street railroad corporation or association is subject to taxation by the cities and towns in which the same are situated. The track, buildings, cars, horses and, if the cars are propelled by electricity, the poles, wires, insulators, dynamos, engines, boilers and machinery owned or used by such corporation or association for the purposes of such railroad shall be valued and assessed like other property in such town. If, however, the track of a horse railroad or the track, wires and poles of an electric railroad are situated in two or more towns, the value per mile of such track, wires and poles shall first be determined by a joint conference of the assessors of all such towns, and so much of the track, poles and wires as are situated in each town shall be therein taxed like other property upon the valuation per mile thus determined. The president, treasurer or secretary of such corporations or associations shall furnish to the assessors of any town in which their track, wires and poles are situated, a statement of the length of such track, wires and poles, when required. The tax hereby provided shall be in place of all other taxes upon said railroad, its property and stock, excepting for its proportion of the salary and expenses of the railroad commissioners as provided in section eighty-six, the amount which each street railroad has to pay under said section eighty-six, shall be deducted from the tax provided by this section, before payment to the town.

If situated in more than one town, how assessed.

Subject to no other taxes.

Personal Property.

SECT. 6. Personal property for purposes of taxation includes goods, chattels, moneys, and effects, wheresoever they are; all vessels at home or abroad; obligations for money or other property; money at interest, and debts due the persons to be taxed more than they are indebted, but not including in such debts or indebtedness any loan on mortgage of real estate, taxable as real estate, except the excess of such loan above the assessed value of the mortgaged real estate; public stocks and securities; shares in moneyed and other corporations within or without the state, except as otherwise provided by law; annuities payable to the person to be taxed, when the capital of such annuities is not taxed in this state; and all other property not taxable as real estate

What personal property is subject to taxation.

Only the excess of mortgage debts above the value of the estate mortgaged, taxable.

Exemptions.

SECT. 7. The following property and polls are exempt from taxation:

I Property of the United States and of this state.

II. The personal property of all literary and scientific institutions; the real and personal property of all benevolent and charitable institutions incorporated by the state; the real estate of all literary and scientific institutions occupied by them for their own purposes, or by any officer thereof as a residence. Corporations whose property or funds in excess of their ordinary expenses are held for the relief of the sick, the poor, or the distressed, or of widows and orphans, or to bury the dead, are benevolent and charitable corporations within the meaning of this specification, without regard to the sources from which such funds are derived, or to limitations in the classes of persons for whose benefit they are applied, except that so much of the real estate of such corporations as is not occupied by them for their own purposes, shall be taxed in the municipality in which it is situated. And any college in this state, authorized under its charter to confer the degree of Bachelor of Arts or of Bachelor of Science, and having real estate liable to taxation, shall, on the payment of

Exemptions.

United States and Maine property.

Property of literary and benevolent institutions exempt from taxation.

Colleges whose estate is liable to taxation, shall be reimbursed by the State.

such tax and proof of the same to the satisfaction of the governor and council be reimbursed from the state **—proviso.** treasury to the amount of the tax so paid ; provided, however, the aggregate amount so reimbursed to any college in any one year shall not exceed fifteen hundred dollars ; and provided, further, that this claim for such reimbursement shall not apply to real estate hereafter bought by any such college.

Household furniture, apparel, tools, &c. III.   The household furniture of each person, not exceeding three hundred dollars to any one family, his wearing apparel, farming utensils, mechanics' tools necessary for his business, and musical instruments not exceeding in value fifteen dollars to one family.   And in addition thereto the beds, bedding and kitchen utensils requisite for each family and a library not exceeding one hundred dollars in value.

Meeting-houses, burial places and parsonages. IV.   Houses of religious worship, including vestries, and the pews and furniture within the same, except for parochial purposes ; tombs and rights of burial ; family burying grounds as described in section seven of chapter fifteen : public cemeteries as provided in section eleven of chapter fifty-five, and property held by a religious society as a parsonage, not exceeding six thousand dollars in value, and from which no rent is received.   But all other property of any religious society, both real and personal, is liable to taxation the same as others' property.

Young animals V.   Mules, horses and neat cattle less than two years old, and swine and sheep less than six months old.

Farm and orch ard products. VI.   Hay, grain and potatoes, orchard products and wool, owned by and in possession of the producer.

Indians and wards. VII.   The polls and estates of Indians ; and the polls of persons under guardianship.

Aged and infirm poor. VIII.   The polls and estates of persons who by reason of age, infirmity or poverty are in the judgment of the assessors unable to contribute toward the public charges.

Highway tax on islands. IX.   The polls and estates of inhabitants of islands on which there are no highways, may be exempted from the highway tax at the discretion of the town to which they belong.

X.   The aqueducts, pipes and conduits of any corpo- Aqueducts, and
ration, supplying a town with water. are exempt from ditionally.
taxation, when such town takes water therefrom for the
extinguishment of fires, without charge. But this exemption does not include therein, the capital stock of —but not the
such corporation. any reservoir or grounds occupied stock, reservoir,
for the same, or any property. real or personal, owned property.
by such company or corporation, other than as herein-
above enumerated.

XI.   Whenever a landholder, having, prior to March Planted forest
thirty, eighteen hundred and eighty-two planted or set empted for
apart for the growth and production of forest trees any twenty years.
cleared land or lands from which the primitive forest
had been removed, successfully cultivates the same for
three years, the trees being not less in numbers than
two thousand on each acre and well distributed over the
same, then, on application of the owner or occupant
thereof to the assessors of the town in which such land
is situated, the same shall be exempt from taxation for
twenty years after said application, *provided*. that said —proviso.
applicant at the same time files with said assessors a
correct plan of such land with a description of its location, and a statement of all the facts in relation to the
growth and cultivation of said incipient forest; *provided
further*, that such grove or plantation of trees is during
that period kept alive and in a thriving condition.

XII.   Mines of gold, silver, or of the baser metals, Mines, for ten
when opened and in process of development, are exempt years.
from taxation for ten years from the time of such opening. But this exemption does not affect the taxation —but not lands
of the lands or the surface improvements of the same, provements.
at the same rate of valuation as similar lands and buildings in the vicinity.

Dogs.

SECT. 8.   Town assessors shall include in the tax Dogs may be
lists of their town all dogs owned by or in possession licensed.
of any inhabitant on the first day of each April, setting
the number and sex thereof opposite the names of the
respective owners or persons in whose possession the
same are found, and shall assess on all dogs over four

—license fees. months old an annual license fee of one dollar for each male, and two dollars for each female dog, to be collected of such owner, or person in possession, in the same manner as state, county and town taxes are collected.

Dogs to be killed if fees not paid.

SECT. 9. If any such license fee remains unpaid ten days after it has been demanded of the person liable, by the collector of taxes, said collector shall issue his warrant directed to any constable of his town commanding him forthwith to destroy the dog for which such license fee was assessed. Any constable receiving such warrant from the collector of taxes of his town shall immediately execute the same by shooting, or by destroying such dog in some other convenient and expeditious manner.

Disposal of moneys accruing from the licensing of dogs to remunerate losses caused by them.

—claim for losses and evidence to sustain it.

SECT. 10. Treasurers of towns shall keep a separate account of all moneys received for such licenses, and of all sums paid out therefrom. Every person suffering loss or damage by reason of the worrying, maiming, or killing of his fowls or domestic animals by a dog not his own, or in his possession, may within ten days after he knows of such loss or damage, present his claim therefor in writing to the municipal officers of the town wherein such loss or damage happens ; and upon satisfactory sworn evidence of the nature and extent thereof, that the claimant has used due diligence to discover the owner of said dog and has not been able to do so, or that the owner of said dog is not financially responsible to the amount of such damage, they shall approve

—duties of town treasurers relating to approved claims for dog damages.

such portion of said claim as they deem just, and shall lodge it with the treasurer who shall register it and, annually on the first day of March, pay the amounts so approved in full, if the gross amount received by the town within the year preceding for such licenses shall be sufficient for that purpose ; otherwise he shall apply such amount *pro rata* in full discharge of such claims. If any portion of said license fees shall remain unexpended as aforesaid at the end of the municipal year, it shall be added to the funds of the town for general purposes.

SECT. 11. The provisions of sections eight, nine and ten shall not be construed as affecting item IV of section fifty-nine of chapter three, nor section one of chapter thirty. *These provisions not to affect other laws respecting dogs.*

Real Estate.

SECT. 12. Taxes on real estate shall be assessed in the town where the estate lies, to the owner or person in possession thereof on the first day of each April. In cases of mortgaged real estate, the mortgagor, for taxation, shall, except as provided in the following section, be deemed the owner, until the mortgagee takes possession, after which the mortgagee shall, except as provided in said section, be deemed the owner. *Real estate where taxable.*

Mortgages of Real Estate.

SECT. 13. When any person has an interest in real estate not exempt from taxation under the provisions of this chapter, as holder of a duly recorded mortgage given to secure the payment of money, the amount of which is fixed and certain, the amount of his interest as mortgagee shall be assessed as real estate in the place where the land lies ; and the mortgagor shall be assessed only for the value of said real estate after deducting the assessed value of all such mortgagee's interests therein. Any mortgagor or mortgagee of real estate may bring in to the assessors of the town where such real estate lies, within such time as shall be specified for bringing in lists as provided in section fifty-one of this chapter, a statement under oath of the amount due on each separate lot or parcel of such real estate, and the name and residence of every holder of an interest therein as a mortgagee or mortgagor. When such property is situated in two or more places, or when a recorded mortgage includes for one sum two or more estates or parts of an estate, an estimate of the amount of the mortgagee's interest in each estate or part of an estate shall be given in such statement. The assessors shall, from such statements or otherwise, ascertain the proportionate parts of such estates that are the interests of mortgagees and mortgagors respectively, and shall *Interests under mortgages of real estate, how taxed.* *—mortgagor or mortgagee may show assessors their interest in mortgaged estate.* *—when mortgaged estate is in two or more places or mortgage includes more than one parcel for one sum.*

assess the same. Whenever, in any case of mortgaged real estate, a statement is not brought in as herein provided, no tax for the then current year on such real estate shall be invalidated for the reason that a mortgagee's interest therein has not been assessed to him. When such property is situated in two or more places, the amount of the mortgagee's interest to be assessed in each place shall be proportioned to the assessed value in the respective places of the mortgaged real estate, deducting therefrom the taxable amount of prior mortgages if any thereon.

SECT. 14. If any holder of such a mortgage fails to file in the assessors' office a full statement as provided in the preceding section, the amount stated in the mortgage shall be conclusive as to the extent of such interest; but the mortgagee's interest in such real estate shall not be assessed at a greater sum than the fair cash valuation of the land and the structures thereon or affixed thereto; and the amount of a mortgage interest in an estate that has been divided after the creation of such mortgage shall not be required to be apportioned upon the several parts of such estate, except as provided in section twenty-six.

SECT. 15. Mortgagors and mortgagees of real estate shall, for the purposes of taxation, be deemed joint owners until the mortgagee takes possession; and until such possession is taken by a first mortgagee, the assessors or the collector of taxes, upon application to any one of them, shall give to any such mortgagee or mortgagor a tax bill showing the whole tax on the mortgaged estate, and the amount included in the valuation thereof as the interest of each mortgagee and of the mortgagor respectively. If the first mortgagee is in possession, he shall be deemed sole owner; and any other mortgagee in possession shall be deemed joint owner with prior mortgagees.

SECT. 16. Deeds of real estate absolute in form but given as security for loans, are, for the purposes of taxation, to be treated as mortgages.

Wood, Bark and Timber under Contract.

SECT. 17.   Whenever the owner of real estate notifies the assessors that any part of the wood, bark and timber standing thereon has been sold by contract in writing. and exhibits to them proper evidence, they shall assess such wood, bark and timber to the purchaser. *Standing wood, bark and timber may be taxed to purchaser.*

SECT. 18.   A lien is created on such wood, bark and timber, for the payment of such taxes ; and may be enforced by the collector by a sale thereof when cut, as provided in section two hundred. *Lien, how enforced.*

SECT. 19.   When a tenant paying rent for real estate is taxed therefor, he may retain out of his rent the taxes paid by him ; unless there is an agreement to the contrary. *Tenant may retain from rent tax paid by him.*

Personal Property, Where Taxable.

SECT. 20.   All personal property within or without the state. except in cases enumerated in the following section, shall be assessed to the owner in the town where he is an inhabitant on the first day of each April. *Personal estate, taxable where owner resides.*

SECT. 21.   The excepted cases referred to in the preceding section are the following : *Exceptions.*

I.   All personal property employed in trade. in the erection of buildings or vessels, or in the mechanic arts, shall be taxed in the town where so employed on the first day of each April ; *provided*, that the owner, his servant, sub-contractor or agent, so employing it, occupies any store, shop, mill, wharf, landing place or ship yard for the purpose of such employment in the town where such property is on said day. *Personal property, used in trade, ship-building or mechanic arts.*

II.   All forest products in transit from the forests and floating in the streams or waters of the state or lying on the banks or shores thereof, when not at the place where they are to be manufactured or employed, are taxable to the owner in the town where he resides. unless previously taxed under section seventeen. *Provided,* That all lumber, logs, timber, lath, pickets, shingles, posts, cord-wood, tan bark, poles for electric wires, or railroad ties, that may be piled or left in any yard, railroad reserve, or in any shed, shall not be *Forest products in transit, where taxable.* *Piled and stored lumber, logs, &c., taxable where situated April 1.*

7

deemed in transit, but shall be assessed to the owner thereof in the town where the same may be situated on the first day of April, unless taxed under section seventeen.

Personal property owned out of the state.

—exceptions.

III. Personal property which, on the first day of each April is within the state, and owned by persons residing out of the state, or by persons unknown; except vessels built, in process of construction, or undergoing repairs, and hides and the leather, the product thereof, when it appears that the hides were sent into the state to be tanned, and to be carried out of the state when tanned; shall be taxed to the person having the same in possession, or to the person owning or occupying any store, shop, mill, wharf, landing, ship yard or other place therein where said property is on said day, and a lien is created on said property in behalf

—lien, in favor of persons paying tax.

of such person, which he may enforce for the re-payment of all sums by him lawfully paid in discharge of

—lien on the property taxed.

the tax. A lien is also created upon the property for the payment of the tax, which may be enforced, by the constable or collector to whom the tax is committed, by a sale of the property, as provided in sections one hundred and ninety-four, two hundred and two, two hundred and one. If any person pays more than his

—remedy for paying more than proportion of tax.

proportionate part of such tax, or if his own goods or property are applied to the payment and discharge of the whole tax, he may recover of the owner such owner's

—owners to furnish assessors where tanneries are located a sworn account of hides and leather on hand, April 1.

proper share thereof. Persons engaged in the tanning of leather in the state, shall on or before the first day of each April, furnish to the assessors of the town where they are carrying on said business, a full account, on oath, of all hides and leather on hand received by them from without the state, and all hides and leather on hand from beasts slaughtered in the state, which last named hides and leather shall be taxed in the town where they were tanned.

Machinery and real estate of corporations.

IV. Machinery employed in any branch of manufacture, goods manufactured or unmanufactured, and real estate belonging to any corporation, except when otherwise expressly provided, shall be assessed to such corporation in the town or place where they are situated or employed; and in assessing stockholders for their

shares in any such corporation, their proportional part
of the value of such machinery, goods and real estate,
shall be deducted from the value of such shares.

V. All mules, horses, neat cattle, sheep and swine
not exempt shall be taxed in the town where they are
kept on the first day of each April, to the owner, or
person who has them in possession at that time. All
such animals, which are in any other town, than that in
which the owner or possessor resides, for pasturing or
any other temporary purpose on said first day of April,
shall be taxed to such owner or possessor in the town
where he resides; and all such animals, which are out
of the state, or in any unincorporated place in the state
on said first day of April, but owned by, or in charge
and possession of any person residing in any town,
shall be taxed to such owner or possessor in the town
where he resides. If a town line so divides a farm that
the dwelling-house is in one town, and the barn or out-
buildings or any part of them is in another, such
animals kept for the use of said farm, shall be taxed in
the town where the house is.

Mules, horses, cattle, sheep and swine, where and to whom to be taxed.

—when town line divides a farm.

VI. Personal property belonging to minors under
guardianship, shall be assessed to the guardian in the
place where he is an inhabitant. The personal property of all other persons under guardianship, shall be
assessed to the guardian in the town where the ward is
an inhabitant.

Personal property of minors and wards.

VII. Personal property held in trust by an executor, administrator, or trustee, the income of which is to
be paid to any other person, shall be assessed to such
executor, administrator, or trustee, in the place where
the person to whom the income is payable, as aforesaid, is an inhabitant. But if the person to whom the
income is payable, as aforesaid, resides out of the state,
such personal property shall be assessed to such executor, administrator, or trustee, in the place where he
resides.

Trust property, where taxable.

VIII. Personal property placed in the hands of any
corporation as an accumulating fund for the future benefit of heirs or other persons, shall be assessed to the
person for whose benefit it is accumulating, if within

Funds intrusted to corporations.

the state, otherwise, to the person so placing it, or his executors, or administrators, until a trustee is appointed to take charge of it or its income, and then to such trustee.

Undistributed personal property, in hands of executors or administrators.

IX.   The personal property of deceased persons in the hands of their executors or administrators not distributed, shall be assessed to the executors or administrators in the town where the deceased last dwelt, until they give notice to the assessors, that said property has been distributed and paid to the persons entitled to receive it.   If the deceased at the time of his death did not reside in the state, such property shall be assessed in the town in which such executors or administrators live.

Of religious societies.

X.   Personal property held by religious societies shall be assessed to the treasurer thereof in the town where they usually hold their meetings.

Property taxed elsewhere.

XI.   Personal property in another state or country on the first day of each April, and legally taxed there.

Stock of toll bridges, how, where and to whom taxed.

SECT. 15.   The stock of toll bridges shall be taxed as personal property, to the owners thereof, in the towns where they reside, except stock owned by persons residing out of the state, which shall be taxed in the town where the bridge is located, and where such bridge is in two towns, one half of such stock so owned by persons residing out of the state shall be assessed and taxed in each town.

Stock of water, gas or electric companies, how taxed.

SECT. 22.   Stock in any local corporation, chartered for the purpose of supplying towns with water, gas, electric lights or power, held by any person unknown, or out of the state, shall be taxed in the town where such corporation is located or transacts its ordinary business, as provided for the taxation of bank stock, in section thirty-six.

Powers of tax officers, are the same as in assessing bank stocks.

SECT. 23.   The powers of assessors, collectors and treasurers, and the liens on the stock, shall be the same as provided in sections thirty-six, thirty-seven, thirty-nine and forty, and the duties therein imposed on cashiers, shall be performed by the treasurers of such corporations.

Clerks failing to make returns,

SECT. 24.   When the clerk of a corporation holding property liable to be taxed, fails to comply with sec-

tiou thirty, chapter forty-six, whether the corporation property deemed corpo-rate.
was chaitered before or since the separation of Maine
from Massachusetts, such property for the purposes of
taxation, shall be deemed corporate property, liable to
be taxed to the corporation, although its stock has been
divided into shares and distributed among any number
of stockholders.

SECT. 25. Such property, both real and personal, is Such property, how taxable.
taxable for state, county. city, town, school district,
and parochial taxes, to be assessed and collected in the
same manner and with the same effect as upon similar
taxable property owned by individuals. If the corpora- —when fran-chise may be sold on warrant of distress.
tion has the right to receive tolls, such right or fran-
chise may be taken and sold on warrant of distress for
payment of such taxes, as such property is taken and
sold on execution.

SECT. 26. Blood animals, brought into the state and Blood animals.
kept for improvement of the breed, shall not be taxed
at a higher rate than stock of the same quality and kind
bred in the state

SECT. 27. When an insuiance or other incorporated Stock of compa-nies invested, how to be taxed.
company is required by law to invest its capital stock
or any part thereof in the stock of a bank, or other corporation in the state, for the security of the public,
such investments shall not be liable to taxation except
to the stockholders of the company so investing as
making a part of the value of their shares in the capital
stock of said company.

SECT. 28. When the capital stock of any insurance Stock of insur-ance companies, when exempt from taxation.
company incorporated in the state, is taxed at its full
value. the securities and pledges held by said company
to the amount of said stock. are exempt from taxation ;
but if the pledge or security consists of real estate in a
town other than that where the stockholder resides, it
shall be taxed where it lies, and the stock shall be
exempt to the amount for which it is assessed.

SECT. 29. When personal property is mortgaged or Mortgaged per-sonal property.
pledged, it shall for purposes of taxation, be deemed
the property of the party who has it in possession, and —distress.
it may be distrained for the tax thereon.

SECT. 30. The undivided real estate of a deceased Real estate of deceased, how taxed.
person may be assessed to his heirs or devisees without

designating any of them by name until they give notice to
the assessors of the division of the estate, and the names
of the several heirs or devisees ; and until such notice
is given, each heir or devisee shall be liable for the
whole of such tax, and may recover of the other heirs
or devisees their portions thereof when paid by him ;
and in an action for that purpose, the undivided shares
of such heirs or devisees in the estate, upon which such
tax has been paid, may be attached on mesne process,
or taken on execution issued on a judgment recovered
in an action therefor.   Or such real estate may be
assessed to the executor or administrator of the deceased, and such assessment shall be collected of him
the same as taxes assessed against him in his private
capacity, and it shall be a charge against the estate and
shall be allowed by the judge of probate ; but when such
executor or administrator notifies the assessors that he
has no funds of the estate to pay such taxes, and gives
them the names of the heirs, and the proportions of
their interests in the estate to the best of his knowledge,
the estate shall no longer be assessed to him.

Personal estate
of partners, how
to be taxed.
SECT. 31.   Partners in business, whether residing in
the same or different towns, may be jointly taxed, under
their partnership name, in the town where their business
is carried on, for all personal property enumerated in
paragraph one of section twenty-one, employed in such
business ; and if they have places of business in two or
more towns, they shall be taxed in each town for the
—exception.
portion of property employed therein ; except that if
any portion of such property is placed, deposited or
situated in a town other than where their place of business is, under the circumstances specified in said paragraph, and paragraph two of said section, they shall be
taxed therefor in such other town ; and in such cases
they shall be jointly and severally liable for such tax.

Lands may be
assessed to
owners or ten-
ants.
SECT. 32.   All real estate, and such as is usually
called real, but is made personal by statute, may be
taxed to the tenant in possession, or to the owner,
whether living in the state or not, in the town where it
is ; and when a state, county or town tax is assessed on
—part owners
may be taxed
and pay, sepa-
rately.
lands owned or claimed to be owned, in common, or in
severalty, any person may furnish the collector, or treas-

urer, to whom the tax is to be paid, an accurate description of his part of the land, in severalty, or his interest, in common, and pay his proportion of such tax; and thereupon his land or interest shall be free of all lien created by such tax.

SECT. 33. When assessors continue to assess real estate to the person to whom it was last assessed, such assessment is valid, although the ownership or occupancy has changed, unless previous notice is given of such change, and of the name of the person to whom it has been transferred or surrendered; and a tenant in common, or joint tenant, may be considered sole owner for the purpose of taxation, unless he notifies the assessors what his interest is.

Assessments may be continued to the same person until notice of transfer.

—tenant in common, shall be considered owner.

SECT. 34. The buildings, lands, and other property of manufacturing, mining and smelting corporations, made personal by their charters, and not exempt from taxation, and all stock used in factories, shall be taxed to the corporation, or to the persons having possession of their property or stock, in the town or place where the corporations are established, or the stock is manufactured; and there shall be a lien for one year on such property and stock for payment of such tax, and it may be sold for payment thereof, as in other cases; and shares of the capital stock of such corporations shall not be taxed to their owners.

Property of manufacturing, mining and smelting corporations, how and where taxed.

—lien for collection.

—shares.

SECT. 35. All real property in the state owned by any bank incorporated by this state, or by any national bank or banking association, shall be taxed in the place where the property is situated, to said bank or banking association, for state, county and municipal taxes, according to its value, like other real estate; but the stock of such banks shall be taxed to the owners thereof where they reside, if known to be residents of the state; but taxation of shares in such banks shall not be at a greater rate than is assessed upon other moneyed capital in the hands of citizens

Real estate of banks, where to be taxed.

—bank stock, where taxed.

SECT. 36. Stock of any bank held by persons out of the state, or unknown, which has not been certified according to section thirty, of chapter forty-six, in any town in the state, and is not there assessed; and the stock of any bank appearing by the books thereof to be

Taxation of bank stock owned out of the state.

held by persons residing out of the state, or whose residence is unknown to the assessors, shall be assessed in the town where such bank is located, or transacts its ordinary business; and such town has a lien on such stock and all dividends thereon, from the date of such assessment, until such tax and all costs and expenses arising in the collection thereof are paid. No assignment, sale, transfer or attachment passes any property in such stock unless the vendee first pays such tax and cost; cashiers of banks shall return to the assessors of the town where such bank is located or transacts its business, all the stock in such bank not returned to the assessors of other towns, according to said section thirty, of chapter forty-six; and such returns shall be made at the time and in the manner prescribed therein, and shall be the basis of taxation of such property.

Cashiers are required to exhibit books.

SECT. 37. The cashier or other officer of each bank, shall exhibit on demand, to the assessors of any town all the books of such bank that contain any record of the stock of such bank or any dividend, declared or paid thereon, and if requested, shall deliver to them a

—to deliver certified copy of record of dividend.

true and certified copy, of so much of said record as they require. Should any cashier neglect or refuse to

—if he refuses, bank to be doomed.

perform the duties required by this and the preceding section, the assessors may doom such bank in such sum as they deem reasonable, and the assessment shall bind the bank, and the tax thereon shall not be abated, and for such neglect or refusal, such cashier forfeits five

—cashier also liable.

hundred dollars to be recovered in an action of debt, half to the prosecutor and half to the state.

Shares to be taxed in the town where bank is located, when residence of holder is unknown or is out of the state.

SECT. 38. When returns of stock in banks and national banking associations and other corporations are made according to the preceding section, or section thirty of chapter forty-six, if it is found by the assessors of any town receiving such returns that the holders of such stock do not reside in such town, they shall within fifteen days return the names of such stockholders, with the amount of stock held by them to the assessors of the town where such stockholders reside, if their residence is known, and within the state; and if not, such return shall be made to the assessors of th town where the bank is located, and shall be subject to section thirty-six of this chapter.

SECT. 39. The collector of a town, to whom has been committed a tax upon the stock of any bank, shall, within thirty days after the bills of assessment are delivered to him, cause a written notice to be delivered to the cashier or president thereof, stating the description of stock taxed, to whom assessed, if stated in the bills, and the tax thereon. No dividend shall be paid on such stock after such notice until the tax and all cost thereon are paid. The cashier may pay such tax, and payment shall constitute a charge in offset against any dividend thereon. Should such tax remain unpaid for ninety days after such notice, the collector may sell such stock in the manner specified in sections two hundred and five and two hundred and six. For the purpose of collecting taxes on bank stock, collectors may act in any town. *Collectors of taxes shall give notice. —no dividend to be paid until tax is paid. —tax charged in offset. —stock may be sold. —powers of collectors extended.*

SECT. 40. Any town treasurer, or his successor in office, may maintain an action on the case against any bank, and recover therein the tax assessed if unpaid, and the lawful charges upon any share thereof, if any dividend thereon has been paid after such tax was assessed; but judgment shall not be rendered in such action for a larger sum in damages than the dividend thus paid, and all such taxes and charges may be recovered in one suit, if said treasurer so elect. *Actions may be maintained by treasurers of towns and cities.*

Assessors' Duties.

SECT. 41. Each assessor or assistant assessor before entering upon the duties of his office, shall take and subscribe the following oath (or affirmation): "I, do solemnly swear (or affirm) that I will appraise all the property subject to taxation in the   of   so far as required by law, equally and at its just value and as I would appraise the same in payment of a just debt due from a solvent debtor, having regard to the current value of such property and the sales thereof other than auction sales in the locality where situated, so help me God (or, under the pains and penalties of perjury)." *Oath of town assessors. —form.*

—oath filed and recorded in town clerk's office.

Said oath shall be administered by the town clerk and filed and recorded in his office.

Assessors to notify inhabitants to bring in sworn inventories of polls and property.

SECT. 42.   Before proceeding to make an assessment, the assessors shall give seasonable notice thereof to the inhabitants of their respective towns in the manner specified in section fifty-one, requiring the inhabitants to prepare and bring in sworn inventories of their polls and all their estates real and personal, whether exempt

—owners must furnish description of real estate.

from taxation or not, of which they were possessed on the first day of April of the same year, describing each parcel of real estate sufficiently to identify it clearly ; also

—and statements of amount due on mortgages of real estate, with name and residence of parties interested.

statements, under oath, by the mortgagors and mortgagees of real estate lying in said town, of the amount due on each separate lot or parcel of such real estate and the name and residence of every holder of an interest therein as mortgagor or mortgagee. and an estimate by any mortgagee of the amount of his interest in any mortgage of real estate situated in two or more places or mortgage including, for one sum, two or more parcels.

Assessors to distribute blanks before April 10th, annually.

—where to be left.

SECT. 43.   Town assessors to whom the blanks as provided by sections sixty-seven and sixty-eight are furnished, shall distribute one copy to each person, corporation and firm liable to taxation in their several towns, by leaving the same, on or before the tenth day of April, annually, with each person so taxable, of full age and not insane or under guardianship, or at the usual place of residence, the office or other place of business of each person, and with a principal officer

—assessors may receive tax payer's statement when leaving notice.

of each taxable corporation ; and the assessor shall, at the time he delivers such blank form, demand and receive such statement, unless such tax payer shall require further time to make out the same, in which case the tax payer shall deliver the same to the assessors, assistant assessors. or to one of them, duly filled out,

—when inventory must be returned to the assessors.

subscribed and sworn to on or before the day specified by the assessors under the provision of section fifty-one.

Blanks to non-residents to be sent by mail.

—non-residents to make sworn return within ten days after receiving blanks

SECT. 44.   If any person liable to taxation in any town or a principal officer of any corporation so liable, resides out of the town, the assessors shall forward to such person or officer, if known, a copy of said blank inventory by mail ; and such person or officer of such corporation shall fill out and complete such inventory

in all respects as herein required, under oath, and return
the same to the assessors within ten days after receiving said blanks.

SECT. 45. Any person or corporation, so liable to *Failing to re-*
taxation in any town, failing to receive such blank *ceive blanks,
tax payer must*
inventory, shall apply to the assessors for a copy of *apply for them
by April 15th,*
such blank on or before the fifteenth day of April and *and return in
ten days.*
shall return the same duly completed within ten days
thereafter. Corporations shall act through their presi- *—corporations.*
dents, secretaries or treasurers under this act.

SECT. 46. Every person or corporation may include *Value may be
stated in lists.*
in said list a statement of the value of any property
therein named. The assessors shall not be bound by *—but assessors
not bound by it.*
said valuation, but shall make such personal examination of all visible property as will enable them to appraise it at its just value.

Tax Payers' Oath.

SECT. 47. The oath required to said inventory may *Oath may be
administered by*
be administered by one of the assessors or assistant *assessors or
assistants, or by*
assessors of said town or by a justice of the peace or *qualified officer.*
other person qualified to administer oaths, and shall be
printed on said inventories as follows :

"I,   of
do solemnly swear (or affirm) that the above is a true, *Form of oath of
tax payer.*
full and correct list and description of all my property,
both real and personal, and that I have set down only
such debts as I am unconditionally bound to pay. to the
amount of deduction claimed and not including debts
secured by mortgages of real estate taxable as such ;
that my answers to these interrogatories are true according to my best knowledge and belief, and that I have
not conveyed or disposed of any property or estate, nor
created any fictitious debt for the purpose of evading
the provisions of law or of affecting the value and
amount of my taxable property. So help me God ; (or
under the pains and penalties of perjury.)"

SECT. 48. In case of property in the possession of *Trust property,
how returned.*
trustees, estates of deceased persons and persons under
guardianship, and of all property not in the care or
possession of the owners, the blank inventory shall be

delivered to or procured by the person to whom the property is by law taxable, who shall fill out, make oath to, and return the same to the assessors.

Penalty for wilful omission to return sworn inventories.

SECT. 49. If a person or corporation wilfully omits to make, swear to and deliver said inventory, or to answer any interrogatory therein, as required by this act, or makes a false answer or statement therein ; then, said assessors shall insert against the name ·"refused to inventory" or "refused to swear or affirm," and shall

—assessors' duties.

ascertain, as best they can, the amount of the taxable property of such person or corporation, shall appraise

—shall appraise at full value and double the same.

the same at its just value and shall double the sum so obtained, and the amount so found shall be the sum on which the tax shall be assessed, and such person or corporation is thereby barred of his right to make appli-

—right of appeal barred to tax payers who wilfully omit to return sworn lists.

cation to the assessors or to the county commissioners for any abatement of such taxes unless such inventory is offered with such application, and satisfactory proof produced that such person or corporation was prevented from returning it at the time required by accident, mis-

—false oath to inventory is perjury.

fortune, or mistake. Any person falsely making oath to such inventory shall be deemed guilty of perjury and punished accordingly. When any person shall be

—persons prevented by sickness or absence have thirty days after recovery or return to file.

unavoidably prevented from making and verifying an inventory of his property for taxation, by sickness or absence. the assessors shall enter against his name "sick" or "absent," and when the assessors shall have fixed the amount thereof, he may at any time within thirty days after his recovery or return, make, verify on oath and file with the assessors. or one of them. his inventory ; but in such case before the assessors shall receive such inventory, the person making the same

—affiant must certify the cause of delay.

shall add to the required affidavit a statement to the effect that his failure to verify and return such statement at the proper time was occasioned by absence or sickness, and the assessors. if satisfied that the same is true and the inventory correct, shall amend their list of of his property accordingly.

Town Assessors' Oath after Assessment.

SECT. 50. All assessors of taxes shall take and subscribe upon the invoices or assessment lists of both resident and non-resident taxes an oath or affirmation to the following effect, which may be administered by the town clerk or any justice of the peace: Oath of town assessors to lists.

"We,   , and   , assessors for the   of   in the county of   , do severally solemnly swear (or affirm) that the value of all property, including moneys, credits, investments in bank stocks, joint stock companies or otherwise, of which a statement has been made to us by the persons required by law to list the same, is truly returned as set forth in such invoice: that in every case where by law we have been required to ascertain the items and value of the property of any person, firm or corporation, we have diligently and by the best means in our power, endeavored to ascertain the same; that, as we verily believe, a full list with the value thereof, estimated by the rules prescribed by law, is set forth in this invoice; and that in no case have we knowingly omitted to demand of any person of whom by law we were required to make such demand, an inventory such as he was required by law to make and return; and each for himself does solemnly swear (or affirm) that he has not in any way connived at any violation or evasion of any of the requirements prescribed by law in relation to the enumeration and valuation of every kind of property subject to taxation." —form of oath.

Whoever falsely takes the foregoing oath shall be deemed guilty of perjury and shall be punished accordingly. —penalty for falsely taking oath.

SECT. 51. The town assessors shall on or before the second Monday in April in each year give reasonable public notice of the times and places where they will be in session for the purpose of receiving inventories of taxable property and of hearing all parties in regard to their liability to taxation. Such notice shall be posted upon the outer door of the town house and of every school-house in towns and plantations, and in cities, on the outer door of every voting place, and in some news- Town assessors to notify tax payers to bring in lists of taxable property. —notices, how posted and published.

paper published in said town or city, if any, and by such other means as the assessors shall deem proper.

Rule for appraisal of property by assessors.

SECT. 52. The assessors shall appraise each item of property, in order to determine its just value, at such sum as they would appraise the same in payment of a just debt due from a solvent debtor, having regard to the current value of such property, and the sales thereof other than auction sales, in the locality where it is situated, and shall, in the assessment lists, describe each parcel of real estate, sufficiently to make its exact location and identity clear.

—assessors must describe real estate.

Assessors, how punished for neglect to deliver or mail blank inventories, or other neglect of duty.

SECT. 53. If any assessor or board of assessors shall neglect to deliver in hand or leave at the residence or place of business of any person, or of an officer, as hereinbefore designated, of a corporation liable to be taxed in their respective towns, or shall fail to mail to any non-residents so liable, the blank inventory provided by this act for returns of property, when such assessor shall have reason to believe such person or corporation to be the owner or custodian of taxable property therein ; or shall wilfully violate any provision of this chapter, or neglect to perform any duty imposed thereby or by any law of the state to which no different penalty is affixed, he or they shall be fined for each offence one hundred dollars to the use of the town, to be recovered by indictment within one year after the commission of the offence. or by an action of debt by the town treasurer brought within two years thereafter.

Penalty for wilful undervaluation of property for taxation.

SECT. 54. Every assessor of any city or town, or other person chosen to determine the valuation of property for the purpose of taxation who shall knowingly fix any such valuation of any property at a less sum than its full and fair cash value in order that the tax payers of such city or town may escape payment of their just proportion of any state or county tax, or for any other fraudulent or corrupt purpose, or who shall knowingly fix the valuation of any such property at a higher sum than its full and fair cash value for the purpose of evading or aiding in the evasion of any law which, at the time such valuation is made, is in force limiting municipal indebtedness or the rate of taxation,

—penalty for corruptly over-valuing property for purpose of evading law limiting town indebtedness.

to a percentage of valuation, or for any other fraudulent, corrupt, or malicious purpose, shall be punished
by a fine not exceeding one thousand dollars, or by
imprisonment not exceeding six months, or by both
such fine and imprisonment.

SECT. 55. The assessors of each town shall make, *Assessors to prepare lists of polls and property by August 1st, annually, noting exemptions.* on or before the first day of August, 1892, and on or before the first day of August annually thereafter, in suitable blank books, true and accurate lists of all the male polls between twenty-one and seventy years of age belonging to such town, whether at home or abroad, distinguishing such as are exempted from taxation, and shall also make true and accurate lists of all property both real and personal, distinguishing such as is exempt by law from state and county taxes within their several towns, and all such property of whatever kind wherever *—what must be included in the lists.* situated subject to taxation therein for the then current year, including cash on hand or on deposit in banks other than savings banks, and debts due or owing from solvent debtors (exceeding the amount owing by the tax payer), also all public and private securities and stocks. And said assessors shall affix to said estates of each individual, firm and corporation set forth in said lists, the full cash value thereof as provided in section fifty-two, and shall also make separate lists of all *—separate lists of vessels, with names, age, value and tonnage.* vessels owned in whole or in part in their respective towns, stating the name, age, value and tonnage thereof, and shall arrange in alphabetical order an abstract of the individual list of all tax payers in such town or city, giving the aggregate valuations of personal and real *—list of aggregates to be prepared for inspection of tax payers.* estate, on or before the first day of August in each year, for the inspection of the tax payers of such town or city ; and said assessors shall, on or before the first day of September, annually, make and return on blank lists which shall be furnished by the state assessors for that pur- *—returns to state assessors of aggregates by September 1st, annually.* pose, aggregates of polls and of the valuation of each and every class of property assessed in their respective towns, with the total valuation and percentage of taxation, and before transmitting the same to the state assessors shall make and subscribe on said aggregates an oath or affirmation, as follows : "We, the assessors *—town assessors to swear to returns to state assessors.* of the   of   , do swear (or affirm) that the foregoing statement contains true aggregates of the valuation of each class of property assessed in said town of   for the year   , and that we have followed all the requirements of law in valuing, listing and returning the same. So help me God" (or "under the pains and penalties of perjury").

—form of oath.

Report on Corporate Property.

Town assessors to report names and property of certain corporations to state assessors.

SECT. 56. The assessors shall annually, on or before the first day of September, return to the state assessors the names of all corporations, except banks of issue and deposit, having a capital stock divided into shares, chartered by the state or organized under the general laws for the purposes of business or profit, and established in their respective towns or owning real estate therein, and of all companies, copartnerships, and other associations having a location or place of business in this state in which the beneficial interest is held in shares assignable without consent of the other associates specifically authorizing such transfer, and a statement in detail of the works, structures, real estate, and machinery owned by each of said corporations, companies, copartnerships, and associations, and situated in such town, with the value thereof, on the first day of April preceding, and the amount at which the same is assessed in said town for the then current year. They shall also. at the same time, return to the state assessors the amount of all taxes laid, or voted to be laid. within said town, for the then current year, for state, county, and town purposes.

—and return amount of all taxes laid within town for current year.

Penalty for neglect.

SECT. 57. If the assessors of a town neglect to comply with the requirements of the preceding section, each assessor so neglecting shall forfeit one hundred dollars.

Supplementary assessments may be made, to correct mistakes.

SECT. 58. When any assessors, after completing the assessment of a tax, discover that they have by mistake omitted any polls or estate liable to be assessed, they may, during their term of office, by a supplement to the invoice and valuation, and the list of assessments, assess such polls and estate their proportion of such tax according to the principles on which the assessment was made, certifying that they were omitted by mistake. Such supplemental assessments shall be committed to the collector with a certificate under the hands of the assessors, stating that they were omitted by mistake, and that the powers in their previous warrant, naming the date of it, are extended thereto ; and the collector has the same power, and is under the same obligations to collect them, as if they had been contained in the original list; and all assessments shall be valid, notwithstanding that by such supplement the whole amount exceeds the sum to be assessed by more than five per cent.

SECT. 59. The assessors shall allow the selectmen, mayor and treasurer of such town or city and the state's attorney for the county to examine the inventory or inventories of any person which they may name, and shall also permit each tax payer or his attorney to examine his or her own inventory or inventories and shall not allow any other person to inspect said inventories. Any or all such inventories shall be lodged in the office of the assessors, and shall be produced in court by one of them upon subpœna for that purpose. The contents of said inventories shall not be disclosed by any person having access to the same, except as set forth in this section and in the event of prosecutions for breach of the provisions of this act. Whoever violates the provisions of this section forfeits one hundred dollars. *Inventories not open to public inspection; who are privileged to examine them.*

—the contents not to be disclosed except as provided in case of prosecution.

—penalty.

SECT. 60. The assessors shall deduct from the debts due, if any, to any tax payer, only so much of his indebtedness as is in excess of the aggregate amount of bonds, stocks and other securities exempt from taxation by the laws of this state and the amount of his deposits in any savings bank, savings institution, or trust company in this state or elsewhere ; and no debt owing shall be taken into consideration in estimating such deduction, unless the person claiming the deduction states in his inventory the amount of such debt, and the name and place of residence of the person to whom it is owing. *Tax payer can have deduction for such debts only as are in excess of his non-taxable securities and deposits.*

—the creditor's name and residence must be disclosed before debt can be deducted.

8

Taxes assessed according to this chapter.

SECT. 61. Except in parishes and societies where different provision is made, all taxes shall be assessed according to the provisions of this chapter.

Liability of assessors for personal faithfulness only.

SECT. 62. Assessors of towns, plantations, school districts, parishes and religious societies, are not responsible for the assessment of any tax, which they are by law required to assess; but the liability shall rest solely with the corporations for whose benefit the tax was assessed, and the assessors shall be responsible only for their own personal faithfulness and integrity.

State Board of Assessors.

Governor to nominate chairman and two associates as board of state assessors.

SECT. 63. The governor shall nominate, and by and with the advice and consent of the council appoint, one officer to be designated chairman of state assessors and two others one of whom shall be taken from each of the two principal political parties to be associate state assessors, the three to be known as the board of state assessors, who shall take and subscribe the oath provided by the constitution of this state, Art IX , Sec. 1, and hold their offices as provided in the following section.

Their term of office.

SECT. 64. The term of office of the chairman of said board shall be for six years and until a successor is appointed and qualified in his place. The term of one of said associate assessors under such first appointment, shall be for four years and of the other for two years, and until another is appointed and qualified in his place. The senior member, after the first appointment, as aforesaid, shall be chairman of the board. Said state assessors shall be appointed within sixty days after the approval of this act, and shall hold their first meeting at the state capitol within thirty days thereafter. The term of appointment of such assessors thereafter shall be for six years, excepting appointments made to fill unexpired terms.

Powers of state assessors to procure evidence.

SECT. 65. Said board of state assessors shall have power to summon before them and examine on oath any town assessor or other officer or person whose testimony they shall deem necessary in the proper discharge of their duties, and may require such witnesses to bring with them, for examination, any records or other public documents in their custody or control which said state assessors may deem necessary for their information in the performance of their duties.

SECT. 66. Any two of said board shall have authority to transact all business appertaining to their office, but all three must be duly notified of each and every meeting for the transaction of business. In case of the death, resignation, refusal, or inability to serve of any one or more of said board, the governor, with advice and consent of the council, shall, as soon as may be, fill such vacancy by appointment, and the assessor so appointed shall hold said office for the balance of the term of the person in whose place he was appointed.

Two a quorum to do business.

—vacancies in the board, how filled.

SECT. 67. The state assessors shall, on or before the first day of April, 1892, and annually thereafter, on or before said day, furnish at the expense of the state, to the assessors of the several towns, blank inventories sufficient in number to meet the requirements of this act, and in most convenient form, with suitable interrogatories. to contain, when filled, a full statement of all taxable property real and personal of each tax payer in said town on the first day of April in said year. Said blanks shall be so formulated by the state assessors as to require, under oath, from each person and corporation such full information as to each class and item of his or its taxable property, real and personal, as will enable the town assessors, after a personal examination of all visible property, to appraise all of such property at its just value in money.

State assessors to furnish blanks to town assessors.

—what the blanks must contain.

SECT. 68. Such inventories shall also contain, when filled, a statement of debts actually due from said tax payers on the first day of April, to the amount of any deduction claimed as an offset to debts due said tax payers ; and no deduction shall be made in the list of any person, by reason of debts owing by him. unless such statement includes the name and place of residence of each creditor to whom he is so indebted and the amount so owing by him to each creditor. No deduction shall be allowed a tax payer on account of his being an indorser or surety for another nor shall any deduction be allowed a tax payer by reason of any joint indebtedness, except to the amount which he would be

Debts owing by tax payers to the amount of deductions claimed from debts due them.

—no deductions allowed to sureties.

—deductions to joint debtors only for their

several proportions of the indebtedness.

obliged to pay if all the persons jointly bound were to pay equal parts of the debt.

A part of this chapter printed on inventory blanks.

SECT. 69. The state assessors shall cause to be printed upon the back of the blank inventories sections six, seven and forty-one to sixty-two both inclusive. of this act.

State assessors to supply blanks for return of aggregate valuations, to town assessors.

SECT. 70. Said state assessors shall seasonably furnish to the town assessors blanks on which to return the aggregates required by section fifty-five, and shall have the required oath printed thereon.

Duties of state assessors.

SECT. 71. Said state assessors shall do and perform all the acts and duties now required by law to be done and performed by the state treasurer as to the assessment of taxes on wild lands ; by the governor and council relating to the assessing and taxing of railroad corporations and associations, and all corporations, companies or persons doing telegraph. telephone or express business within the state, and shall assess all taxes upon corporate franchises.

To report to governor and council annually by December 1st.

SECT. 72. The state assessors shall annually before the first day of December, make a report to the governor and council of their proceedings and shall include therein a tabular statement of all statistics derived from returns from local assessors, with schedules of all corporations on which state taxes were assessed during

—more detailed tabular statements required biennially.

the year, and, for the years in which they shall equalize the valuation of the state, their report shall include tabular statements of the state valuation by towns and counties.

State equalization board.

SECT. 73. Said state assessors shall constitute a state board of equalization whose duty it shall be to equalize the state tax among the several towns, to fix the valuation of real and personal estate on which the state and county taxes shall be levied in each town ; and to perform the duties heretofore devolving upon the legislature in the apportioning of the state taxes among the several towns of the state.

State assessors to visit counties biennially to secure information and investigate charges relating to taxation.

SECT. 74. Said state assessors shall visit officially every county in the state at least once in two years, and shall there sit at such times and places as they may deem necessary to secure information to enable them to make a just and equal assessment of the valuation of the taxable property in any place therein, and to investigate charges of concealment of property liable to assessment. Said assessors shall give such public notice of their sessions as they may deem proper.

SECT. 75   Said s'ate assessors shall be provided with suitable rooms in the state house, and shall be furnished by the secretary of state with necessary books, blanks, stationery, printing, notices and summonses, and may employ such clerical assistance as they shall deem necessary, the expenses for which shall be audited by the governor and council.

State assessors to be furnished with rooms, stationery, &c.

—may employ clerks.

—expenses.

SECT. 76.   A statement of the amount of the assessed valuation for each town, after adjustment as provided by section seventy-eight, the aggregate amount for each county, and for the entire state as fixed by the board of equalization, shall be certified by said board and deposited in the office of the secretary of state as soon as completed, and before the first day of December preceding the regular sessions of the legislature. The valuation thus determined shall be the basis for the computation and apportionment of the state and county taxes, until the next biennial assessment and equalization.

Equalizing board to file aggregates in office of secretary of state by December 1st, annually.

—basis for state and county taxes.

SECT. 77.   Said state assessors shall be held to a constant attendance upon the duties of their office ; shall be vigilant and prompt in the correcting and equalizing of valuations and in the investigation of charges of concealed property liable to assessment.   Said state assessors shall receive a salary of two thousand dollars each, and for necessary expenses in the performance of their duties such sum as shall be allowed by the governor and council on properly itemized accounts.

State assessors, vigilance required. Their salaries.

—expense accounts to be audited by governor and council.

SECT. 78.   Said state assessors shall equalize and adjust the assessment list of each town, by adding to or deducting from it or any part thereof, such amount as, when compared with valuations in other towns shall equalize the same ; and said lists after they have been so equalized shall constitute the general list of the state upon which state and county taxes shall be assessed.

Their powers in relation to town assessments.

SECT. 79.   If the assessors of any town, or one of them, shall fail to appear before said board of equalization or to transmit to them the lists hereinbefore named

If no lists are returned by town assessors to board of equalization,

valuation how fixed. within ten days after the mailing or publication of notice or notices to them, to so appear or transmit said lists, the said board may in its discretion report the valuation of the estates and property and lists of polls liable to taxation in the town so in default, as it shall deem just and equitable.

Wild lands to be returned by land agent with value and description. SECT. 80. The land agent shall prepare and deliver to said state assessors full and accurate lists of all townships or parts of townships or lots or parcels of wild lands in this state sold and not included in the tax lists, whether conveyed or not, with the fair value thereof, and shall lay before said state assessors all information in his possession touching the value and description of wild lands at their request; also a state-

—statement of timber permits, with value, to be returned. ment of all lands on which timber has been sold or a permit to cut timber has been granted by lease or otherwise, with the fair value thereof. All other state officers, when requested, shall in like manner lay all information in their possession, touching said valuation before said state assessors.

State Taxes.

Treasurer of state shall issue warrants for state tax. SECT. 81. When a state tax is ordered by the legislature, the treasurer of state shall forthwith send his warrants directed to municipal officers of each town or other place, requiring them to assess upon the polls and estates of each, its proportion of such state tax for the current year; and shall in like manner send like warrants for the state tax for the succeeding year, forthwith upon the expiration of one year from the time such

—tax for each year shall be separately ordered. tax is so ordered. The tax for each year shall be separately ordered and apportioned; and the amount of such proportion shall be stated in the warrants.

What state treasurer's warrant shall require. SECT. 82. The treasurer, in his warrant, shall require said officers to make a fair list of their assessments, setting forth in distinct columns against each person's name, how much he is assessed for polls, how much for real estate, and how much for personal estate, distinguishing any sum assessed to such person as guardian, or for any estate in his possession as executor, administrator, or trustee; to insert in such list the number of

acres of land assessed to each non-resident proprietor,
and the value at which they have estimated them; to
commit such list, when completed and signed by a
majority of them, to the collector or constables of such
town or other place, with their warrants in due form,
requiring them to collect and pay the same to the treasurer of state, at such times as the legislature, in the act
authorizing such tax, directed them to be paid; and to
return a certificate of the names of such officers, and the
amount so committed to each, one month at least before
the time at which they are required to pay in such tax.

State Taxation of Railroads.

SECT. 83. Every steam railroad company, incorpo- Annual returns
rated under the laws of the State, or doing business _{of railroad} companies.
therein, shall annually, between the first and fifteenth
days of April, return to the secretary of state under
oath of its treasurer, the amount of the capital stock of
the corporation, the number and par value of the
shares, and a complete list of its shareholders, with
their places of residence and the number of shares
belonging to each on said first day of April. The
returns shall also contain a statement of the whole —to state length
length of its line, the length of its line within the state, _{of line and} assessed value
and the assessed value in each town of its stations and _{of stations, &c.}
other property taxed by municipalities.

SECT. 84. Every corporation, person or association, Corporations or
operating any such railroad in the state, shall pay to _{persons operat-} _{ing railroads}
the treasurer of state, for the state, an annual excise _{shall pay annu-} _{al excise tax.}
tax, for the privilege of exercising its franchises in the
state, which, with the tax provided for in sections four
and eighty-six, is in place of all taxes upon such railroad, its property and stock. There shall be appor- —state shall
tioned and paid by the state from the taxes received _{pay cities and} _{towns one per}
under this and the following section, to the several _{cent. on stock} _{held therein.}
cities and towns, in which on the first day of April in
each year, is held railroad stock exempted from other
taxation, an amount equal to one per cent. on the value
of such stock on that day, as determined by the state
assessors; *provided, however*, that the total amount —proviso.
thus apportioned on account of any railroad shall not

exceed the sum received by the state as tax on account of such railroad ; and *provided further*, that there shall not be apportioned on account of any railroad and its several parts, if any, operated by lease or otherwise, a greater part of the whole tax received from such railroad and its several parts, than the proportion which the amount of capital stock of such railroad and its several parts owned in this state bears to the whole amount of the capital stock of said railroad and its several parts.

Amount of tax, how to be ascertained.

SECT. 85. The amount of such annual excise tax shall be ascertained as follows : the amount of the gross transportation receipts as returned to the railroad commissioners for the year ending on the thirtieth day of September preceding the levying of such tax, shall be divided by the number of miles of railroad operated, to ascertain the average gross receipts per mile ; when such average receipts per mile do not exceed two thousand two hundred and fifty dollars, the tax shall be equal to one quarter of one per cent. of the gross transportation receipts ; when the average receipts per mile exceed two thousand two hundred and fifty dollars and do not exceed three thousand dollars, the tax shall be equal to one-half of one per cent. of the gross receipts ; and so on increasing the rate of the tax one-quarter of one per cent. for each additional seven hundred and fifty dollars of average gross receipts per mile or fractional part thereof.

—railroads partly outside the state, tax upon, how to be ascertained.

When a railroad lies partly within and partly without the state, or is operated as a part of a line or system extending beyond the state, the tax shall be equal to the same proportion of the gross receipts in the state, as herein provided, and its amount shall be determined as follows : the gross transportation receipts of such railroad, line or system, as the case may be, over its whole extent, within and without the state, shall be divided by the total number of miles operated to obtain the average gross receipts per mile, and the gross receipts in the state shall be taken to be the average gross receipts per mile multiplied by the number of miles operated within the state.

Steam railroad companies taxed for sala-

SECT. 86. In addition to all other taxes now provided by law, every corporation operating a railroad shall pay to the state treasurer such a sum as shall be ries and expenses of its *pro rata* part of the amount of the salary and ex- railroad commissioners. penses of the railroad commissioners and of their clerk, to be determined as provided in the foregoing section for computing the annual excise tax on steam railroads.

SECT. 87.   The state assessors, on or before the first Tax, how fixed; notice to day of each April, shall determine the amount of such companies. taxes and report the same to the treasurer of state, who shall forthwith give notice thereof to the corporation, person or association, upon which the taxes are levied.

SECT. 88   Said taxes shall be payable, one-half on Tax, payable in July and the first day of July next after the levy is made, and the October. other half on the first day of October following.   If any party fails to pay the taxes as hereinbefore required, the treasurer of state may proceed to collect the same, —treasurer shall enforce with interest, at the rate of ten per cent. a year, by collection. action of debt, in the name of the State.   Said taxes —tax to be a lien and take shall be a lien on the railroad operated, and take prece- precedence dence of all other liens and incumbrances.

SECT. 89.   Any corporation, person or association Aggrieved parties may aggrieved by the action of the state assessors in deter- apply for abatement to mining the taxes through error or mistake in calculat- state assessors. ing the same, may apply for abatement of any such excessive taxes within the year for which such taxes are assessed, and if, upon re-hearing and re-examina- tion, the taxes appear to be excessive through such error or mistake, the state assessors may thereupon abate such excess, and the amount so abated shall be deducted from any tax due and unpaid, upon the rail- road upon which the excessive tax was assessed ; or, if there is no such unpaid tax, the governor shall draw his warrant for the abatement, to be paid from any money in the treasury not otherwise appropriated.

SECT. 90.   If the returns required by law, in relation Further returns may be required to railroads, are found insufficient to furnish the basis by railroad commissioners. upon which the taxes are to be levied, the railroad com- missioners shall require such additional facts in the returns as may be found necessary ; and, until such returns are so required. or, in default of such returns when required, the state assessors shall act upon the best information that they may obtain.   The railroad

—railroad commissioners shall have access to books of railroad companies.

commissioners shall have access to the books of railroad companies, to ascertain if the required returns are correctly made ; and any railroad corporation, association, or person operating any railroad in the state, which refuses or neglects to make the returns required by law, or to exhibit to the railroad commissioners its books for the purposes aforesaid, or makes returns

—penalty for refusing to make returns, or for making false ones.

which the president, clerk, treasurer, or other person certifying to such returns knows to be false, forfeits not less than one thousand, nor more than ten thousand dollars, to be recovered by indictment, or by an action of debt in any county into which the railroad operated extends.

Taxation of Sleeping Cars.

What are included as sleeping cars.

SECT. 91.   Every joint-stock association, company or corporation, incorporated under the laws of any other state and conveying to, from and through this state or any part thereof, passengers and travelers in palace cars, drawing-room cars, parlor cars, sleeping cars or chair cars, on contract with any railroad company. or the manager, lessee, agent or receiver thereof, shall be held and deemed to be a sleeping car company.

—returns to state assessors required, of sleeping car companies doing business in this state.

Every such sleeping car company doing business in this state shall annually, between the first day of April and the first day of June, report to the state assessors, under oath of an officer or agent of such corporation, the gross amount of all its receipts within or without the state for fares earned or business done by such company within this state for the year then next preceding the said first day of April ; and in computing such gross receipts the same shall be in the proportion that the distance travelled in this state bears to the

—tax of two dollars per one hundred dollars of gross receipts.

whole distance paid for.   At the time of making such report, such company shall pay into the treasury of the state the sum of two dollars on every one hundred dollars of such gross receipts.   Every sleeping car

—penalties for failure to report and pay tax.

company failing or refusing, for more than thirty days after the first of June, to render an accurate account of such gross receipts, as above provided, and to pay the required tax thereon, forfeits twenty-five dollars

for each additional day such report and payment shall
be delayed, to be recovered in the name of the state of
Maine, at the instance of the state treasurer, in any
court of competent jurisdiction, and the attorney general shall conduct such suit; and such sleeping car
company so failing or refusing shall be prohibited from
carrying on such business until such payment is made.
All railroad companies in this state, or the persons —railroad
managing or operating the same, are prohibited from prohibited from
hauling any cars of any sleeping car company while so companies in
in default, and for each violation of this prohibition default.
shall be liable to pay to the state of Maine the sum of —penalty.
one hundred dollars, to be recovered in the proper
action instituted by the attorney general in the name
of the state, at the request of the state treasurer.

Telegraph Companies.

SECT. 92. Every telegraph corporation, company, or Taxation of
person doing business within the state shall annually companies, 2½
pay into the state treasury a tax of two and a half per *per cent. ad*
cent. on the value of any telegraph line owned by said *valorem.*
corporation, company or person within the state, including all poles, wires, insulators, office furniture,
batteries and instruments, whether owned or leased.   ·

SECT. 93. Every such corporation, company or Returns to
person shall annually, on or before the fifteenth day of state assessors.
April, return to the state assessors, under oath of its
superintendent, the amount and value of all the prop-·
erty enumerated in the preceding section, owned or
leased by it within the limits aforesaid, with the names
and residences of all shareholders in the state, and the
number of shares owned by each on the first day of
April annually, together with the number of shares
owned by non-residents, and the state assessors shall
determine said values and assess said tax thereon by
the first day of May annually. Said state assessors
shall thereupon certify said assessment to the state
treasurer who shall forthwith notify the several parties
assessed.

SECT. 94. Said tax shall be paid into the treasury When tax must
on or before the first day of September, annually, and be paid to state.

is in place of all state or municipal taxation on any of
the property or shares of said corporations, companies
\or persons.

Telephone Companies.

**Taxation of
telephone
companies,
two and one-
half per cent.
ad valorem on
property
owned.**

SECT. 95. Every telephone corporation, company or
person doing business within the state, shall annually
pay into the state treasury a tax of two and a half per
cent. on the value of any telephone line owned by said
corporation. company or person. within the state, including all poles, wires, insulators, transmitters, telephones, batteries. instruments, telephonic apparatus
and office furniture ; and also a tax of two and a half
per cent. on the value of any such telephones or other
telephonic apparatus or patent of any description used
but not owned by such corporation. company or
person, and under lease from or subject to the payment
of royalty for its use to any corporation or person
beyond the limits of this state.

**—same on prop-
erty subject to
royalty or lease.**

**Returns to state
assessors.**

SECT. 96. Every such corporation, company or person shall annually on or before the fifteenth day of
April, return to the state assessors under oath of its
superintendent, the number of telephones, batteries and
instruments, the amount, and value of all the property
enumerated in the preceding section, owned or leased
by it within the limits aforesaid, on the first day of
April, annually, and the state assessors shall determine
said values and assess said tax thereon by the first day
of May annually. The state assessors shall thereupon
certify said assessment to the state treasurer, who shall
forthwith notify the several parties assessed. Said tax
shall be paid into the treasury on or before the first day
of September, annually, and is in place of all state or
municipal taxation on any property or shares of said
corporations, companies or persons and on any property
so leased by them. Taxes paid on leased instruments
or property may be charged by the corporation, company or person against the sum payable for the use or
royalty of the same.

**—exemption
from other
taxes.**

**Penalty for
neglect.**

SECT. 97. Any corporation, company or person neglecting to make the returns required by sections ninety-
three and ninety-six, forfeits twenty-five dollars for

every day's neglect, to be recovered by an action of debt in the name of the state.

Express Companies.

SECT. 98. Every express corporation, company or person doing express business on any railroad, steamboat or vessel in the state, shall, annually, before the first day of May, apply to the treasurer of state for a license authorizing the carrying on of said business; and every such corporation, company or person shall annually pay to the treasurer of state, three-fourths of one per cent. of the gross receipts of said business for the year ending on the first day of April preceding. Said three-fourths of one per cent. shall be on all of said business done in the state, including a *pro rata* part on all express business coming from other states or countries into this state, and on all going from this state to other states or countries.

Taxation of express companies.

—must have license from state treasurer, annually.

—tax on gross receipts.

SECT. 99. Every such corporation, company or person shall, by its properly authorized agent or officer, annually, on or before the fifteenth day of May, make a return under oath to the state assessors, stating the amount of said receipts for all express matters carried within the state as specified in the preceding section, including such *pro rata*; whereupon the state assessors shall on or before the first day of June following, assess the tax therein provided, and forthwith certify the same to the treasurer of state, who shall thereupon notify said corporations or companies or persons, and said taxes shall be paid into the state treasury on or before the first day of September following.

Returns to state assessors required by May 15th, annually.

—when tax must be paid.

SECT. 100. The tax assessed upon express corporations or companies and persons as aforesaid, is in place of all local taxation, except that real estate owned by such corporations or companies or persons shall be taxed in the municipality where the same is situated, as non-resident real estate.

Exemption from all other taxes, except on real estate locally taxed.

SECT. 101. Any corporation, company or person neglecting to make returns according to section ninety-nine, forfeits twenty-five dollars for every day's neglect, to be recovered by action of debt in the name of the state.

Penalty for neglect.

Taxation of Collateral Inheritances.

Collateral inheritance tax imposed.

SECT. 102. All property within the jurisdiction of this state, and any interest therein, whether belonging to inhabitants of this state or not, and whether tangible or intangible, which shall pass by will or by the intestate laws of this state, or by deed, grant, sale, or gift made or intended to take effect in possession or enjoyment after the death of the grantor, to any person in trust or otherwise, other than to or for the use of the father, mother, husband, wife, lineal descendant, adopted child, the lineal descendant of any adopted child, the wife or widow of a son, or the husband of the daughter of a decedent, shall be liable to a tax of two and a half per centum of its value, above the sum of five hundred dollars, for the use of the state, and all administrators, executors, and trustees, and any such grantee under a conveyance made during the grantor's life shall be liable for all such taxes, with lawful interest as hereinafter provided, until the same shall have been paid as hereinafter directed

Tax on remainder man how ascertained.

SECT. 103. When any person shall bequeath or devise any property to or for the use of father, mother, husband, wife, lineal descendant, an adopted child, the lineal descendant of any adopted child, the wife or widow of a son, or the husband of a daughter during life or for a term of years, and the remainder to a collateral heir, or to a stranger to the blood, the value of the prior estate shall, within sixty days after the death of the testator, be appraised in the manner hereinafter provided, and deducted, together with the sum of five hundred dollars, from the appraised value of such property, and said tax on the remainder shall be payable within one year from the death of said testator, and, together with any interest that may accrue on the same, be and remain a lien on said property till paid to the state.

On legacy to executor or trustee.

SECT. 104. Whenever a decedent appoints one or more executors or trustees, and in lieu of their allowance makes a bequest or devise of property to them which would otherwise be liable to said tax, or appoints them his residuary legatees, and said bequests, devises, or residuary legacies exceed what would be a reasonable compensation for their services, such excess shall be liable to such tax, and the court of probate having jurisdiction of their accounts shall determine what shall be such reasonable compensation.

SECT. 105. All taxes imposed by this act shall be payable to the treasurer of state by the executors, administrators, or trustees within one year from the death of said testator, or intestate, or the qualification of said trustee ; and if the same are not so paid, interest at the rate of nine per centum shall be charged them and collected from the time said tax became due. *Tax, when payable.*

SECT. 106. Any administrator, executor, or trustee, having in charge or trust any property subject to such tax, shall deduct the tax therefrom, or shall collect the tax thereon from the legatee or person entitled to said property, and he shall not deliver any specific legacy or property subject to said tax to any person until he has collected the tax thereon. *Administrator, etc., to collect or retain tax.*

SECT. 107. Whenever any legacies subject to said tax shall be charged upon or payable out of any real estate, the heir or devisee, before paying the same, shall deduct said tax therefrom and pay it to the executor, administrator, or trustee, and the same shall remain a charge upon said real estate until it is paid ; and payment thereof shall be enforced by the executor, administrator, or trustee, in the same manner as the payment of the legacy itself could be enforced. *Tax on legacy charged on real estate.*

SECT. 108. If any such legacy be given in money to any person for a limited period, such administrator, executor, or trustee shall retain the tax on the whole amount ; but if it be not in money, he shall make an application to the judge of probate having jurisdiction of his accounts to make an apportionment, if the case require it, of the sum to be paid into his hands by such legatee on account of said tax and for such further order as the case may require. *Tax on estate for years.*

SECT. 109. All administrators, executors, and trustees shall have power to sell so much of the estate of the deceased as will enable them to pay said tax in the same manner as they may be empowered to do for the payment of his debts. *Sale of estate to pay tax.*

Inventory of estate subject to tax to be sent state treasurer.

SECT. 110. A copy of the inventory of every estate, any part of which may be subject to a tax under the provisions of sections one hundred and two to one hundred and eighteen inclusive, or if the same can be conveniently separated, then a copy of such part of such inventory with the appraisal thereof, shall be sent by mail by the register or the judge of the court of probate in which such inventory is filed, to the state assessors within ten days after the same is filed. The fees for such copy shall be paid by the executor, administrator, or trustee, and allowed in his account.

Duty of executor, etc., as to real estate becoming subject to tax.

SECT. 111. Whenever any of the real estate of a decedent shall so pass to another person as to become subject to said tax, the executor, administrator, or trustee of the decedent shall inform the state assessors thereof within six months after he has assumed the duties of his trust, or if the fact is not known to him within that time, then within one month after it does become so known to him.

Refunding over-paid tax.

SECT. 112. Whenever for any reason the devisee, legatee, or heir who has paid any such tax shall refund any portion of the property on which it was paid, or it shall be judicially determined that the whole or any part of such tax ought not to have been paid, said tax, or the due proportional part of said tax, shall be paid back to him by the executor, administrator, or trustee.

SECT. 113. The value of such property as may be

Value of property, how ascertained.

subject to said tax shall be its actual market value as found by the judge of probate ; but the state assessors, or any person interested in the succession to said prop-

—appraisal provided for.

erty, may apply to the judge of probate having jurisdiction of the estate, and on such application the judge shall appoint three disinterested persons, who, being first sworn, shall view and appraise such property at its actual market value for the purposes of said tax, and shall make return thereof to said probate court, which return may be accepted by said court in the same manner as the original inventory of such estate is accepted, and if so accepted it shall be binding upon the person by whom this tax is to be paid, and upon the state. And the fees of the appraisers shall be fixed

—appraisers' fees.

by the judge of probate, and paid by the executor,

administrator, or trustee. In case of an annuity or —annuities, how valued.
life estate the value thereof shall be determined by the
so called actuaries' combined experience tables and five
per centum compound interest.

SECT. 114. The court of probate, having either Probate court jurisdiction of
principal or ancillary jurisdiction of the settlement of tax questions
the estate of the decedent, shall have jurisdiction to touching devises and
hear and determine all questions in relation to said tax inheritances.
that may arise affecting any devise, legacy, or inheritance under this act, subject to appeal as in other
cases, and the attorney general shall represent the
interests of the state in any such proceedings.

SECT. 115. Every judge of probate shall, as often Probate judge to return to
as once in six months, render to the state assessors a state assessors
statement of the property within the jurisdiction of his semi-annually property in his
court that has become subject to said tax during such jurisdiction sub-
period, the name of the testator, intestate or grantor ject to such tax.
and the name of the beneficiary whose estate is so taxable. and amount of such taxes as will accrue during
the next six months, so far as the same can be determined from the probate records, and the number and
amount of such taxes as are due and unpaid.

SECT. 116. The fees of judges or registers of probate Fees of judges and registers
for the duties required of them by this act shall be, for of probate.
each order, appointment, decree, judgment, or approval
of appraisal or report required hereunder, fifty cents ;
and for copies of records, the fees that are now allowed
by law for the same. And the administrators, executors, trustees, or other persons paying said tax shall be
entitled to deduct the amount of all such fees paid to
the judge or register of probate from the amount of
said tax to be paid to the treasurer of state.

SECT. 117. No final settlement of the account of any Taxes must be paid before final
executor, administrator, or trustee shall be accepted or settlement of
allowed by any judge of probate unless it shall show, executor, &c., allowed.
and the judge of said court shall find, that all taxes,
imposed by the provisions of this act, upon any property
or interest therein belonging to the estate to be settled
by said account, shall have been paid, and the receipt
of the treasurer of state for such tax shall be the proper
voucher for such payment.

Construction of words.

SECT. 118.   In the foregoing sections relating to collateral inheritances the word "person" shall be construed to include bodies corporate as well as natural persons; the word "property" shall be construed to include both real and personal estate, and any form of interest therein whatsoever, including annuities.

Insurance Companies.

Taxation of foreign insurance and surety companies.

SECT. 119.   Every insurance company or association and surety company which does business in the state, not incorporated or associated under its laws, shall, as hereinafter provided, annually pay a tax upon the gross amount of all premiums received, whether in cash or in notes absolutely payable, on contracts made in the state for insurance of life, property or interests or contracts of guaranty therein at the rate of two per cent. a year;

—proviso, deduction of unearned premiums.

provided however, that so much of any of said premiums as may have been returned during the year to the insured or person guaranteed, as not earned, shall first be deducted from said gross amount; and *provided further*, that nothing in this section shall be so construed as to allow dividends in scrip or otherwise in stock, mutual or mixed companies to be considered return premiums.

Returns to insurance commission required.

SECT. 120.   Every company or association and surety company which by the preceding section is required to pay a tax, shall, on or before the thirty-first day of each January, make a return under oath, to the insurance commissioner, stating the amount of all premiums received by said company, either in cash or notes absolutely payable, during the year ending on the thirty-first day of December previous, also the amount to be deducted therefrom, under the preceding section, specifying the whole amount thereof, and the amount

—state assessors to assess the taxes by April 1st.

of each deduction and to whom paid.   Said tax shall be assessed by the state assessors on or before the first day of June, upon the certificate of the insurance commissioner, to be seasonably furnished therefor, the same to be paid on or before the first day of July following.

—state treasurer to notify companies of assessment.

The state treasurer shall notify the several companies of the assessment, and unless the same is paid as aforesaid, the commissioner shall suspend the right of the company to do any further business in the state until the tax is paid.

SECT. 121. If any insurance company, association or surety company refuses or neglects to make the return required by the preceding section, the state assessors shall make such assessment on such company or association as they deem just, and unless the same is paid on demand, such company or association shall do no more business in the state, and the insurance commissioner shall give notice accordingly. Whoever, after such notice, does business in the state for such company or association. is liable to the penalty provided in section seventy-three of chapter forty-nine. *Company neglecting to make returns, state assessors to fix tax.* *—failure to pay forfeits right to do business in the state.*

SECT. 122. Any insurance company incorporated by a state or country whose laws impose upon insurance companies chartered by this state any greater tax than is herein provided, shall pay the same tax upon business done by it in this state, in place of the tax above provided; and the insurance commissioner may require the return upon which such tax may be assessed to be made to him, and the state assessors shall assess such tax; and if it is not paid as provided in section one hundred and twenty the insurance commissioner shall suspend the right of said company to do business in this state. *Reciprocal taxation provided.*

Unlicensed Insurance Companies.

SECT. 123. No person shall act as an inspector of property for any insurance company or association of companies, of this state, or of any other state or country not licensed to do business in Maine, until he has received a license therefor from the insurance commissioner, authorizing him as representative of the company stated, to inspect property for said company; and such license shall continue until the first day of the next January and may be renewed from year to year if the insurance commissioner deem it advisable. For each such license or renewal the insurance commissioner shall receive twenty dollars for the state. If any person without first giving such bond and receiving such license inspects any property for any such unauthorized company *Inspectors of unlicensed companies must have license to represent their companies in this state.* *—license fee.* *—penalty for inspection without license from*

Insurance
commissioner.

or association of companies or offers to make such inspection upon solicitation of the owners of property or persons in possession thereof or otherwise, or in any way performs the work of an inspector or solicitor of insurance risks, he shall be punished by a fine not exceeding five hundred dollars or by imprisonment not exceeding sixty days for each offence, the fine to be recovered as provided in section eighty-four of chapter forty-nine.

Inspector to
make sworn
return to insur-
ance commis-
sioner annually.

SECT. 124. Each inspector shall keep a correct account of all property by him inspected, and, on or before the thirty-first day of January of each year make a sworn statement and return to the insurance commissioner upon blanks provided by said commissioner, of all property insured by the company or companies he represents, based upon his inspections, for the year

—what it must
contain.

ending December thirty-first preceding, with the amount of insurance written thereon, the company or companies in which insured, and the amount received by said company or companies as premiums.

Inspector to
give bonds.

SECT. 125. Every such inspector before receiving a license shall be required to give bond to the insurance commissioner for the state in such sum and with such

—conditions of
bond.

sureties resident in this state as the insurance commissioner may approve, conditioned for the faithful performance of his duties as prescribed by this act and for the payment of all taxes assessed against the company or companies he represents, in case such company or companies neglect to pay said taxes within the time provided.

Domestic Life Insurance Companies.

Taxation of life
insurance com-
panies.

SECT. 126. Every life insurance company or association organized under the laws of this state, in lieu of all other taxation shall be taxed as follows: First, its

—real estate
locally taxed.

real estate shall be taxed in the town in which such real estate is situated, like other real estate therein.

—on gross
amount of
premiums and
surplus, two per
cent. after de-
ducting value of
real estate.

Second, it shall pay to the state treasurer, for the state a tax of two per cent. upon all premiums, whether in cash or notes absolutely payable, received from residents of this state during the year preceding the assessment, as hereinafter provided. Third, it shall pay to

the state treasurer for the state a tax of three-fourths
of one per cent. per annum on its surplus computed
according to the laws of this state, after deducting the
value of its real estate in this state as fixed in deter-
mining such surplus. Said surplus shall be determined
by the insurance commissioner, and his certificate thereof to the state assessors shall be final, and said assessors
shall assess said taxes on such premiums and surplus.

SECT. 127. Every such company shall include. in its
annual return to the insurance commissioner, a statement of the gross amount of premiums as provided in
the preceding section, and of the real estate held by it
in this state on the thirty-first day of December preceding

SECT. 128. Sections one hundred and twenty and
one hundred and twenty-one, so far as not inconsistent
herewith shall apply to such companies or associations.

Returns to
insurance
commissioner.

Sections 120 &
121 applicable.

Savings Banks and Trust Companies.

SECT. 129. Every savings bank, institution for savings and trust and loan association incorporated under
the laws of the state shall, semi-annually, on or before
the second Mondays of May and November, make a
return to the state assessors. signed and sworn to by its
treasurer, of the average amount of its deposits and
accumulations for the six months preceding each of said
days, deducting an amount equal to the amount of United
States bonds and shares of corporation stocks such as
are by law of this state free from taxation to the stockholders and the assessed value of real estate owned by
said bank, institution or association, together with a
statement in detail of its loans, investments and deposits
within and without the state in separate columns with
aggregates. For wilfully making a false return, the corporation treasurer forfeits not less than five hundred
nor more than five thousand dollars. Such treasurer
shall pay to the treasurer of state a tax on account of
its deposits and accumulations as follows: On so
much of such funds as is loaned to persons resident
or corporations located and doing business in this state,
and so much as is invested in securities of this state

Taxation of
savings banks
and trust and
loan associa-
tions.

—returns to
state assessors,
semi-annually.

—penalty for
making false
return.

—tax payable to
treasurer of
state.

public or private, or on hand or deposited by said banks or associations in this state one-half of one per cent. a year; and on so much of said funds as are loaned, invested or deposited otherwise, one per cent.

Tax, how to be assessed.

SECT. 130. One-half of said tax shall be assessed on the average amount on deposit or invested or loaned including accumulations, for the six months ending on and including the last Saturday in April, and the other half on such average for the six months ending on and

—how appropriated.

including the last Saturday in October. One-half of the sum so paid shall be appropriated for schools, in the manner provided for tax on banks of circulation, in section one hundred and seventeen of chapter eleven,

—when payable.

and one-half to the state, and such taxes shall be paid semi-annually on or before the last Saturdays of May and November.

Deposits are exempt from municipal taxation; but not land held by bank.

SECT. 131. All deposits and accumulations in savings banks in the state are exempt from municipal taxation to the bank or to the depositor, but real estate owned by the bank, not held as collateral security, may be taxed by the town in which the same is located.

Return of bank stock pledged as collateral, shall be made to assessors of municipalities where owners reside.

SECT. 132. Treasurers of savings banks, on the first day of each April shall return to the assessors of towns, where persons reside who own bank stock which is pledged or transferred to said bank as collateral security for loans, the names of persons pledging or transferring such stock and the amount of the same; and stock so pledged or transferred by persons residing out of the state shall be returned by such treasurers in the same manner to the assessors of the town in which the bank whose stock is so pledged or transferred is located. For the purposes of taxation, bank stock so pledged or transferred shall be deemed the property of the persons so pledging or transferring it.

Taxation of Companies When no Returns Have Been Made.

SECT. 133. If any corporation, company or person State assessors to tax companies in absence of returns, fails to make the returns required by sections ninety-three, ninety-six or ninety-nine, the state assessors double assessment. shall make an assessment of state tax upon such corporation, company or person on such valuation, or on such gross receipts thereof, as the case may be, as they think just, with such evidence as they may obtain, and shall double the amount thereof, and such assessment shall be final. If any corporation, company or person —remedies for enforcing payment of state taxes. fails to pay the taxes required or imposed by sections ninety-two, ninety-five, ninety-eight or one hundred and twenty-nine, the treasurer of state shall forthwith commence an action of debt, in the name of the state, for the recovery of the same with interest. In addition to other remedies for the collection of state taxes upon any corporation, such taxes with interest may be recovered by an action of debt, or an action on the case, in the name of the state.

Taxation of Corporate Franchises.

SECT. 134. Every corporation, company or associa- A tax provided for certain corporate franchises. tion, now or hereafter chartered by the legislature or organized under the general laws of the state for purposes of business or profit in the state, or without the state and having an office or place of business in the state for the direction of its affairs or for the transfer of its shares, and having a capital divided into shares, except manufacturing, mining and quarrying corpora- —exceptions. tions, transportation, telegraph and telephone companies, banking corporations, and corporations for supplying heat, light, water or power, operating within the state, and other corporations now subject to an annual state tax, shall pay to the state treasurer on the first day of July, annually, a franchise tax of one-tenth of one per cent. upon its capital stock at the par there- —rate of tax imposed. of ; *provided*, however, that the assessed valuation of property taxed within the state as belonging to any

corporation subject to said franchise tax, shall be
deducted from the amount of its capital stock and said
franchise tax shall be assessed upon the balance.

Returns to be
made to state
assessors annu-
ally by Jan. 1st. SECT. 135.   The clerk or other officer having the
custody of the records of any corporation subject to the
franchise tax provided by the preceding section, shall
by the first day of January, annually, make return to
state assessors showing the principal place of business of
said corporation, its officers and their several places of
residence. its capital stock, with the par value of the
shares, whether paid in or not paid in, and the assessed
valuation of all its property taxed within the state and
where taxed.

SECT. 136.   All officers of any such corporation and
other persons assuming to represent it in the state by
having charge of its affairs or books of account, record
or transfer of its shares, shall severally be personally
liable for the amount of the tax imposed upon such corporation under section one hundred and thirty-four, if
the same is not paid as therein required.   Any such
—corporation
failing to make
returns or pay
tax, forfeits cor-
porate rights. corporation failing to make such return or to pay such
tax within six months after it shall have become due,
forfeits all its corporate rights and franchises.   *Pro-*
vided, however, that such officers, on application to the
state assessors, and satisfactory proof that such corporation has ceased to do business or in any way to exercise its corporate rights or franchises, and after its
charter and corporate powers shall have become forfeited under the provisions of this act, may be relieved
of their liability to pay said tax.

Enrolment and Organization Taxes.

Tax imposed on
corporate char-
ters and articles
of association. SECT. 137.   Every corporation whether chartered by
act of legislature or organized under a general law,
shall, before the enrolment of its act of incorporation,
or the recording in the office of the secretary of state of
its certificate of organization or articles of association,
pay to the treasurer for the use of the state an enrolment or organization tax as follows :   When the specified amount of capital of such corporation does not
exceed five thousand dollars, the sum of twenty-five

dollars; when more than five thousand and not exceeding ten thousand dollars, the sum of fifty dollars; when more than ten thousand and not exceeding twenty thousand dollars, the sum of one hundred dollars; when more than twenty thousand and not exceeding forty thousand dollars, the sum of one hundred and fifty dollars: when more than forty thousand and not exceeding one hundred thousand dollars, the sum of two hundred dollars; and for each fifty thousand dollars or major fraction thereof above one hundred thousand dollars, the sum of one hundred dollars. Any increase in the capital stock of any corporation after its original charter or organization, shall be subject to tax in like proportion, and this provision shall apply to all corporations in existence when this act takes effect. In default of payment as aforesaid, within six months after the approval of such act of incorporation, or of such organization, if under a general law, by the proper officer or officers, such act of incorporation or such organization, shall be null and void. The taxes provided by the foregoing section are in lieu of all fees heretofore provided by law upon the organization of corporations. *—increase of capital stock subject to like tax.* *—forfeiture for non-payment of taxes.* *—exemption from fees.*

SECT. 138. The foregoing section shall not apply to societies incorporated under chapter fifty-five.

Other Private or Special Acts of Legislature.

SECT 139. No private or special act of the legislature other than those specified in section one hundred and thirty-seven, shall be enrolled in the office of the secretary of state, or have the force and effect of law, until the party or parties requesting the passage of such act shall have paid into the state treasury the following sums, to wit; on every act authorizing the division of a county. city or town, the erection of a toll bridge, the extension of a wharf into tide waters, the erection of a road or bridge across tide waters, the construction of a boom or the maintenance of a steam ferry, the sum of fifty dollars; on every other private and special act not hereinbefore enumerated, including all acts amendatory of and additional to other private and special acts, the sum of ten dollars. *A tax on other private or special acts provided.* *—amount of tax.*

Taxation of Lands in Places not Incorporated.

State tax on lands in places not incorporated.

SECT. 140. Lands not exempt, and not liable to be assessed in any town, shall be taxed by the legislature for a just proportion of all state and county taxes as herein provided for ordering the state and county taxes upon property liable to be assessed in towns, and shall be valued and inventoried by the state assessors for that purpose.

Such lands are subject to county taxes.

SECT. 141. Such lands may be assessed by the county commissioners according to the last valuation by the state assessors for a due proportion of county taxes. Lists of such taxes shall immediately be certified and transmitted by the county treasurer to the treasurer of state. In the list. each such township and tract shall be

—treasurer of county to certify lists of such taxes to treasurer of state, who shall give credit for the amount thereof.

sufficiently described, with the date, and amount of assessment on each. The treasurer of state shall, in his books, credit the county treasurer for the amount of each such assessment; and when paid to him, shall certify to the county treasurer the amount of tax and interest so paid, on the first Monday of each January.

Lists of assessments shall be certified and advertised annually.

SECT. 142. When the legislature assesses such state tax, the treasurer of state shall, within three months thereafter, cause the lists of such assessments, with the lists of any county tax so certified to him, both for the current year, to be advertised for three weeks successively in the state paper, and in some newspaper, if any, printed in the county in which the land lies, and shall cause like advertisement of the lists of such state and county taxes for the following year to be made within three months after one year from such assessment. Said

—such lands are held for the payment of taxes.

lands are held to the state for payment of such state and county taxes, with interest thereon at the rate of twenty per cent., to commence upon the taxes for the year in which such assessment is made at the expiration of one year and upon the taxes for the following year upon the expiration of two years from the date of such assessment.

Lands shall be forfeited in one year, if taxes are not paid.

SECT. 143. Owners of the lands so assessed and advertised, may redeem them, by paying to the treasurer of state the taxes with interest thereon, within one year from the time when such interest commences. Each owner may pay for his interest in any tract, whether in common or not, and shall receive a certificate from the treasurer of state, discharging the tax upon the number of acres, or interest, upon which such payment is made. Each part or interest of every such township or tract, upon which the state or county taxes so advertised are not paid with interest within the time limited in this section for such redemption, shall be wholly forfeited to the state, and vest therein free of any claims by any former owner.

SECT. 144. Lands thus forfeited shall. annually in September, be sold by the treasurer of state at public auction to the highest bidder; but never at a price less than the full amount due thereon for such unpaid state and county taxes, interest, and cost of advertising. Notice of the sale shall be given by publishing a list of the lands to be sold with the amount of such unpaid taxes, interest, and costs on each parcel, and the time and place of sale, in the state paper, and in some newspaper, if any, printed in the county in which the lands lie, three weeks successively. within three months before the time of sale.

Treasurer of state shall sell forfeited lands at auction in September annually.

—notice shall be published in some county paper.

SECT 145. If any such tract is sold for more than the amount due, the surplus shall be held by the state to be paid to the owner, whose right has been so forfeited, upon proof of ownership produced to the governor and council.

Surplus shall be paid to owners.

SECT. 146. Any owner may redeem his interest in such lands, by paying to the treasurer of state his part of the sums due at any time before sale; or after sale, by paying or tendering to the purchaser, within a year, his proportion of what the purchaser paid therefor at the sale, with interest at the rate of twenty per cent. a year from the time of sale, and one dollar for a release; and the purchaser, on reasonable demand, shall execute such release; and if he refuses or neglects. a bill in equity may be maintained to compel him, with costs and any damages occasioned by such refusal or neglect. Or such owner may redeem his interest by paying as aforesaid to the treasurer of state, who, on payment of fifty cents, shall give a certificate thereof; which certi-

Owner may pay tax before sale, or he may redeem from the purchaser within one year.

ficate, recorded in the registry of deeds in the county
where the lands lie, shall be a release of such interest,
and the title thereto shall revert and be held as if no
such sale had been made. The governor and council
may draw their warrant on the treasurer for any money
so paid to him, in favor of the purchaser for whom it
was paid, or his legal representatives.

Copy of record
of treasurer's
doings is made
evidence.

—costs
apportioned.

—county taxes
shall be paid
over to county
treasurer.

SECT. 147. The printer's bills for advertising such
lands shall be divided in each case by the number of
townships and tracts advertised, and each shall be
charged with its proportion thereof. All amounts of
county taxes and interest so received by the treasurer
of state, shall be credited by him to the counties to
which they belong, and paid to the treasurers thereof.
The treasurer of state shall record his doings in every
such sale ; and a certified copy of such record shall be
prima facie evidence, in any court, of the facts therein
set forth. He shall give a deed to the purchaser conveying all the interest of the state in the land sold.

Owner may pay
taxes to county
treasurer.

SECT. 148. Any owner of lands so assessed by the
county commissioners for county taxes, may redeem
them by paying to the county treasurer the amount due
thereon for such taxes, interest and charges, and
depositing with the treasurer of state the county treasurer's certificate of such payment, at any time before
the sale.

Assessment on
lands for open-
ing roads in
unincorporated
places.

—lien created.

—when assess-
ment appears
oppressive, an
equitable
amount may be
assessed on
county.

—appeal to S.
J. court.

SECT. 149. When a road is laid over lands under
section forty-one. of chapter eighteen, the county commissioners shall at their first regular session thereafter
assess thereon and on adjoining townships benefited
thereby, such an amount as they judge necessary for
making, opening and paying expenses attending it ; and
such assessment shall create a lien thereon for the payment thereof ; and they may make as many divisions
as are equitable, conforming as nearly as is convenient
to known divisions and separate ownerships, and may
assess upon each a sum proportional to the value thereof
and the benefits likely to result to the same by the estab-
lishment of the road ; when such assessment would be
unreasonably burdensome to such owners, they shall
assess an equitable sum on the county and the balance
only on such land. Any person aggrieved by an assess-

ment may appeal to the supreme judicial court at the —proceedings.
term thereof first held after such assessment; and the
presiding judge at that term shall, on hearing the case,
determine what part of said assessment shall be paid by
the owners of the tract or township, and what part, if
any, by the county, and there shall be no appeal from
such decision. They shall, at the same time, fix the
time for making and opening such road, not exceeding —agent to be appointed to
two years from the date of the assessment, and appoint superintend building of
an agent or agents, not memb rs of their board. to roads.
superintend the same, who shall give bond to the treasurer of the county, with sureties approved by them, to
expend the money faithfully, and to render account
thereof on demand; and they shall publish a list of the
townships and tracts of land so assessed, with the sum
assessed on each, and the time in which the road is to
be made and opened, in the state paper, and in some paper,
if any, printed in the county where the lands lie, three
weeks successively, the last publication to be within three
months from the date of the assessment.

SECT. 150. If the owners make and open such road Owners may discharge their
to the acceptance of the commissioners, after an actual assessments by
examination by one or more of their board, within said building roads.
time, the assessment shall thereby be discharged; otherwise it shall be enforced as hereinafter provided, and
the agents shall proceed immediately to make and
open it.

SECT. 151. Said county commissioners, in Septem- Commissioners annually to
ber, annually, by one or more of their board, shall make inspect county
an inspection of all county roads and other roads origi- roads in unin-corporated
nally located as town roads in the unincorporated town- places.
ships and tracts of land in their counties, and shall
thereupon make an estimate of the amount needed to
put them in repair, so as to be safe and convenient for
public travel, and assess such amount thereon; and they —to make esti-mate of repairs.
shall make as many divisions as are equitable, conform-
ing as nearly as is convenient to known divisions and —divisions and
separate ownerships, and shall assess upon each a sum assessments.
proportionate to the value thereof; and cause so much —to cause
thereof as they deem necessary for the purpose aforesaid, expenditures within one year.
to be expended on said roads within one year thereafter,
which assessment shall create a lien thereon for the pay-

ment thereof ; when such assessment would be unreasonably burdensome to such owners, they shall assess an
equitable sum on the county and the balance only on such
—when burden- lands. They shall make such assessment by the first day
some to owners,
equitable sum to of each January, and at the same time appoint an agent
be assessed on
county. or agents, not members of their board, to superintend
—an agent to be the expenditure thereof, who shall give bonds as pro-
appointed to
superintend the vided in section one hundred and forty-nine ; and they
repair of roads.
shall publish a list of the townships and tracts of land
so assessed, with the sums so assessed on each, and the
roads on which it is to be expended, in the state paper,
—lists of town- and in some paper, if any, printed in the county where
ships and lands
assessed, to be the lands lie, three weeks successively, the last publi-
published.
cation to be within three months from the date of the
assessment.

Land owners SECT. 152. If by the fifteenth of June following,
may discharge
their assessment the owners of such lands repair such roads to the
by repairing
road. acceptance of the commissioners, after an actual examination by one or more of their board, the assessment
shall be thereby discharged ; otherwise it shall be
enforced as hereinafter provided, and the agents shall
proceed immediately to repair such roads.

Proceedings if SECT. 153. If any owner fails to pay the sum so
owner fails to
discharge his assessed on his land, for the expenses of making and
assessment.
opening such new roads, within two months from the
time fixed therefor as provided in section one hundred
and fifty, or fails within two months after the fifteenth
day of each June, to pay his assessment for repairing
roads, as provided in the two preceding sections, the
county treasurer shall proceed to sell the lands so
assessed, by advertising the lists of unpaid taxes. with
the date of assessment, and the time and place of sale,
in the state paper, and in some paper, if any, printed
in the county where the lands lie, three weeks successively, the last publication to be at least thirty days
before the time of sale. No bid shall be received at
such sale for less than the amount due for the tax,
costs and interest at twenty per cent. a year from the
time prescribed for the payment of said tax ; and the
treasurer shall sell so much of such land as is necessary
to pay the unpaid tax, costs and interest as aforesaid,

and give a deed thereof to the purchaser, if any ; and
if no one becomes a purchaser at such sale, it shall be
forfeited to the county ; and such owner or part owner
or tenant in common may redeem his interest therein at
any time within two years from the sale or forfeiture,
by paying to the purchaser or the county the sum for
which it was sold or forfeited, with interest at twenty
per cent. a year, and any sums subsequently paid for
state and county taxes thereon. Any owner of lands —owners
entitled to over-
so sold, shall receive his share in any overplus of the plus.
proceeds of such sale, on exhibiting to the treasurer
satisfactory evidence of his title. In addition to the —additional
remedy.
method provided in this section for the collection of
highway taxes assessed for the purposes named therein,
the county commissioners of any county, may, in writing
at any time subsequent to that when the lands so
assessed might be sold for non-payment of the taxes
assessed therein, direct the treasurer of such county to
commence an action of debt in the name of the inhabitants of said county, against the party liable to pay
such taxes. But no such defendant shall be liable for
any costs of suit in such action unless it appears by the
declaration and proof, that payment of said tax had
been duly demanded by said treasurer before the suit
was commenced.

SECT. 154. In any trial at law or in equity involving *Prima facie*
proof of title by
the validity of any sale or forfeiture of such lands, as purchase at
such sale.
provided in the preceding section, it shall be prima
facie proof of title for the party claiming under it, to
produce in evidence the county treasurer's deed, duly
executed and recorded, the assessments signed by the
county commissioners and certified by them or their
clerk to the county treasurer, and to prove that the
county treasurer complied with the requirements of law
in advertising and selling. But the purchaser or the —lien on land
sold, for taxes,
county shall have a lien on the land sold or forfeited costs and interest.
for the taxes, costs and interest, and any subsequent
taxes legally assessed thereon and paid by either, or
those claiming under them ; and such sums shall be
paid or tendered, before any person shall commence,
maintain or defend any suit at law or in equity, involv-

ing the title to such lands under such sale or forfeiture, notwithstanding any irregularities or omissions in such sale or forfeiture.

County commissioners may repair county roads and bridges in unincorporated places in case of sudden injury.

SECT. 155. County commissioners, in case of sudden injury to county roads and bridges in unincorporated townships and tracts of land in their counties, may cause them to be repaired forthwith, or as soon as they deem necessary, and may appoint an agent or agents not members of their own board, to superintend the expenditure therefor, who shall give bond as required in section one hundred and forty-nine, if required, the whole expense whereof shall be added to their next assessment on said lands for repairs, authorized by section one hundred and fifty, which assessment shall create a lien upon said lands for the whole amount thereof as effectually as is now provided in relation to repairs on such county roads. That portion of said assessment which is for repairs of sudden injuries as aforesaid, shall be set down, in the assessment, in distinct items, in a separate column, and shall not be discharged, under section one hundred and fifty-two, but shall be enforced as is provided in section one hundred and fifty-three.

—agent to give bond.

—assessment for repairs, how made.

—assessments to be itemized.

Purchasers acquire state's title only, and have no claim on the state.

SECT. 156. Purchasers of land sold for non-payment of state and county taxes, and assessments for opening, making and repairing roads, have no claim against the state or county for any defect in the title under such sale, notwithstanding any irregularities in the proceedings, or failure to comply with the law under which the sales were made. Deeds given pursuant to sales made for non-payment of state and county taxes, vest in the grantee the title of the state, or of the county, to the lands sold, subject to the conditions of sale, and no more.

Part owner may redeem his share.

SECT. 157. Any person having a legal interest in a tract so advertised, sold or forfeited, may redeem his interest by paying within the times prescribed, the amount so required to discharge the claim thereon. The rate of interest upon unpaid state and county taxes, and taxes assessed by county commissioners for opening, making and repairing roads, shall be twenty per cent .

commencing at the expiration of one year from the date
of the assessments, except when otherwise provided.

Assessment of Taxes in Incorporated Places.

SECT. 158. When a state tax is imposed and required
to be assessed by the proper officers of towns, the treasurer of state shall send such warrants, as he is, from
time to time, ordered to issue for the assessment thereof,
to the sheriffs, who shall transmit them to the assessors
of the towns in their counties, according to the direc-
tions thereof. *Treasurer of state to send warrants to sheriffs for assessment on towns of state tax.*

SECT. 159. In order to assess a county tax, county
commissioners, at their regular session next before the
first day of each January in which the legislature meets,
shall prepare estimates of the sums necessary to defray
the expenses which have accrued or may probably accrue
for one year from said day, including the building and
repairing of jails, court houses, and appurtenances, with
the debts owed by their counties, and like estimates for
the succeeding year, and the county tax for both said
years shall be granted by the legislature separately at
the same session. *County commissioners to make annual estimates for county taxes.*

SECT. 160. Said estimates shall be recorded by their
clerk in a book ; and a copy thereof shall be signed by
the chairman of the county commissioners, and attested
by their clerk, who shall transmit it to the office of the
secretary of state, on or before the first day of each
January in which the legislature meets, to be by him
laid before the legislature. *Estimates to be recorded and transmitted to secretary of state.*

SECT. 161. When a county tax is authorized, the
county commissioners shall in March in the year for
which such tax is granted, apportion it upon the towns
and other places according to the last state valuation,
and issue their warrant to the assessors, requiring them
forthwith to assess the sum apportioned to their town
or place, and to commit their assessment to the constable
or collector for collection. *County commissioners to apportion sums to be assessed, and to issue warrants to assessors.*

SECT. 162. No assessment of a tax by a town or
parish is legal, unless the sum assessed is raised by vote
of the voters, at a meeting legally called and notified. *Not legal, unless raised at legal meeting.*

10

Applications for Abatements.

Abatements, how applied for and when. SECT. 163. Any person, corporation or firm, having complied with all the requirements of this act relating to the inventory and return of property for taxation, may, within thirty days after notice of the amount of his or their tax, make written application to the assessors for any abatement claimed, stating the grounds of such claim. The assessors shall keep in suitable book form a record of such abatements, with the reasons for each, and report the same to the town at its next annual meeting, and to the mayor and aldermen of cities, by the first Monday in the following March.

Appeal to county commissioners. SECT. 164. If they refuse to make the abatement asked for, the applicant may apply to the county commissioners at their next meeting, and if they think that he is overrated, he shall be relieved by them, and be *—proceedings thereon.* re-imbursed out of the town treasury the amount of their abatement, with incidental charges. The commissioners may require the assessors or town clerk to produce the valuation, by which the assessment was made, or a copy of it. If the applicant fails. the commissioners shall allow the costs to the town, taxed as in a suit in the supreme judicial court, and issue their warrant of distress for collection thereof against him.

Assessments, how made. SECT. 165. The assessors shall assess upon the polls and estates in their town all town taxes and their due proportion of any state or county tax, according to the rules in the latest act for raising a state tax, and in this *—lists, to whom committed.* chapter; make perfect lists thereof under their hands; and commit the same to the constable or collector of their town, if any, otherwise to the sheriff of the county or his deputy, with a warrant under their hands, in the form hereinafter prescribed.

State and county taxes to be added. SECT. 166. They may add their proportion of the state and county tax to any of their other taxes, and make one warrant and their certificates accordingly.

Overlay not to exceed five per cent. SECT. 167. They may assess on the estates such sum above the sum committed to them to assess, not exceeding five per cent. thereof, as a fractional division renders convenient, and certify that fact to their town treasurer.

Sect. 168. They shall make a record of their assessment and of the invoice and valuation from which it was made ; and before the taxes are committed to the officer for collection, they shall deposit it, or a copy of it, in the assessors' office, if any, otherwise with the town clerk, there to remain ; and any place, where the assessors usually meet to transact business and keep their papers or books, shall be considered their office. *Record of assessment and invoice, to be deposited in assessors' office.*

Sect. 169. When they have assessed any county tax and committed it to the officer for collection, they shall return to the county treasurer a certificate thereof with the name of such officer. When they have so assessed and committed a state tax, they shall return a like certificate to the treasurer of state ; and if this is not done, and any part of such tax remains unpaid for sixty days after the time fixed for its payment, the treasurer of state shall issue his warrant to the sheriff or his deputy to collect the sum unpaid of the inhabitants of the town or place. *Certificate to be sent to county treasurer.* *—and to treasurer of state.* *—who shall issue warrant.*

Sect. 170. If any town having less than two thousand inhabitants by the last preceding census does not choose assessors, or if so many of them refuse to accept, that there are not such a number as such town voted to have, the selectmen shall be the assessors, and each of them shall be sworn as an assessor ; and each selectman and assessor shall be paid for his services two dollars for every day necessarily employed in the service of the town. *Selectmen to be assessors in certain events* *—per diem, $2.*

Sect. 171. Any town having less than two thousand inhabitants as aforesaid, neglecting to choose selectmen or assessors, and any other town neglecting to choose assessors, forfeits to the state not exceeding three hundred, nor less than one hundred dollars, as the supreme judicial court orders, on proper complaint by any inhabitant or party interested. *Penalty for neglect to choose.*

Sect. 172. In such case, and when the selectmen or assessors chosen by a town do not accept the trust, the county commissioners may appoint three or more suitable persons in the county, to be assessors of taxes, and such assessors, being duly sworn, shall assess upon the polls and estates in the town their due proportion *When no assessors, county commissioners may appoint.*

of state and county taxes and said penalty, and not
exceeding two dollars a day each, for their own reasonable charges for time and expense in said service ; and
shall issue a warrant under their hands for collecting
the same, and transmit a certificate thereof to the treasurer of state, with the name of the person to whom it
is committed ; and the assessors shall be paid their
charges as allowed by said commissions out of the state
treasury.

—proceedings
thereon.

Such assessors
to obey warrants.

SECT. 173.   All assessors, chosen or appointed as
above provided, shall observe all warrants, received by
them while in office, from the treasurer of state or the
county commissioners of their county.

Penalty for neglect to make
assessments of
state tax.

SECT. 174.   If assessors of a town refuse or neglect
to assess any state tax apportioned on it, and required
by the state treasurer's warrant to be assessed by them,
they forfeit to the state the full sum mentioned in such
warrant ; and such treasurer shall issue his warrant to
the sheriff of the county to levy said sum by distress
and sale of their real and personal estate.

Penalty for neglect to assess
county tax.

SECT. 175.   If such assessors neglect to assess the
county tax required in the warrant of the county commissioners to be assessed by them, they forfeit that sum
to the county ; and it shall be levied by sale of their
real and personal estate, by virtue of a warrant issued
by the county treasurer to the sheriff of the county for
that purpose.

Assessors may
be arrested.

SECT. 176.   If the sheriff cannot find property of
said assessors to satisfy the sum due on either of said
warrants, he may arrest and imprison them, until they
pay the same ; and the county commissioners shall forth-

—other assessors may be
appointed.

with appoint other proper persons to be assessors of
such state and county taxes, who shall be sworn, and
perform the same duties, and be liable to the same penalties, as the former assessors.

Towns neglecting for five
months to
assess, treasurer to issue
warrant to
sheriff to collect.

SECT. 177.   If the inhabitants of a town of which a
state tax is required, neglect for five months, after
having received the state treasurer's warrant for assessing it, to choose assessors to assess it, and cause the
assessment thereof to be certified to such treasurer for
the time being, he shall issue his warrant, under his

hand. to the sheriff of the same county, who shall proceed to levy such sums on the real and personal property of any inhabitants of such town, observing the regulations provided for satisfying warrants against deficient collectors, as hereinafter prescribed. But if the assessors thereof, within sixty days from the receipt of a copy of such warrant from the officer. deliver to him a certificate, according to law, of the assessment of the taxes required by the warrant, and pay him his legal fees, he shall forthwith transmit the certificate to the state treasurer, and return the warrant unsatisfied.

SECT. 178   If the inhabitants of a town of which a county tax is required, neglect to choose and keep in office assessors to assess it, as the law requires, the county treasurer, for the time being, after five months from the time when they received the county commissioners' warrant for assessing it, shall issue his warrant to the sheriff, requiring him to levy and collect the sum mentioned therein ; and he shall execute it, observing the regulations and subject to the condition provided in the preceding section. *For like neglect county treasurer to issue warrant.*

SECT. 179.   If the voters of a town, of which a state or county tax is required, choose assessors who neglect to assess the tax required by the warrant issued to them, or to re-assess the tax on the failure of a collector, and to certify it as the law directs ; and if the estates of such assessors are insufficient to pay such taxes as already provided, the treasurer of state, or of the county as the case may be, for the time being, shall issue his warrant to the sheriff of such county, requiring him to levy, by distress and sale, such deficiency on the real and personal estates of such inhabitants ; and the sheriff or his deputy shall execute such warrants observing all the provisions mentioned in section one hundred and seventy-seven *Warrants to be issued to collect of inhabitants, if not collected of assessors.*

SECT. 180.   Any assessor, chosen and notified to take the oath of office. unreasonably refusing to be sworn, forfeits to the town fifteen dollars, to be recovered by their treasurer in an action of debt ; and the selectmen shall forthwith call a town meeting to fill the vacancy. *Penalty on assessors for refusing to be sworn.* *—vacancy, how filled.*

Assessment of Taxes in Plantations.

Plantations taxed, invested with power of towns for such purpose.
SECT. 181. All plantations required to pay any part of the public taxes, are vested with the same power as towns, so far as relates to the choice of clerk, assessors and collectors of taxes ; and any person, chosen assessor therein, and refusing to accept, or to take the legal oath, after due notice, is liable to the same penalty, to be recovered in the manner mentioned in the preceding section ; and the other assessors shall forthwith call a plantation meeting to fill the vacancy.

And subject to same penalties.
SECT. 182. If any such plantation neglects to choose a clerk, assessors, and collector of taxes, or if the assessors chosen neglect their duty, it shall be subject to the same penalties and proceeded against in the same manner as towns deficient in the same respect.

Officers to be sworn.
SECT. 183. The clerk, assessors, and collectors, shall be sworn as similar officers chosen by a town, and shall receive the same compensation, unless otherwise agreed.

When a tax is laid on a place not incorporated, county commissioners may cause it to be organized as a plantation.
SECT. 184. When a state or county tax is laid on a place not incorporated or organized, the treasurer of state or county commissioners of that county may cause the same to be organized as provided in chapter three, sections seventy-one and seventy-two, for the organization of plantations ascertained to contain two hundred and fifty inhabitants. If the inhabitant to whom the warrant is directed, fails to perform the duties required of him, he forfeits the sums due for state and county taxes, to be recovered by the treasurer to whom the tax is payable.

Assessors to make list of polls, &c.
SECT. 185. The assessors shall thereupon take a list of the ratable polls, and a valuation of the estates of the inhabitants of the plantation, and proceed to assess taxes and cause the same to be collected as required by law.

Laws applicable.
SECT. 186. All laws applicable to organized plantations apply to plantations organized under section one hundred and eighty-four.

Neglect to be sworn.
SECT. 187. Plantation officers neglecting to be sworn when notified, are liable to the same penalties as town officers so neglecting, to be recovered in the same man_

ner. The word *towns* in this chapter including cities and plantations.

Collection of Taxes in Incorporated Places.

SECT. 188. Towns, at their annual meetings, may determine when the lists named in section one hundred and sixty-five shall be committed, and when their taxes shall be payable, and that interest shall be collected thereafter. Towns may fix time for payment, and require interest after.

SECT. 189. The rate of such interest, not exceeding one per cent. a month, shall be specified in the vote, and shall be added to, and become part of the taxes. Not to exceed one per cent. a month.

SECT. 190. The warrant to be issued by selectmen or assessors for collection of state taxes shall be in substance, as follows: Form of warrant for collection of state taxes.

"——, ss. A. B., constable or collector of the town of——, within the county of—— :   GREETING:

In the name of the State of Maine, you are hereby required to levy and collect of each of the several persons named in the list herewith committed unto you, his respective proportion therein set down, of the sum total of such list, it being said town's proportion of the state tax for the year 18   ; and to transmit and pay the same to —— ——, treasurer of state, or to his successor in office, and to complete and make an account of your collections of the whole sum on or before the ——day of——next. And if any person refuses or neglects to pay the sum which he is assessed in said list, you shall distrain his goods or chattels to the value thereof; and keep the distress so taken for four days at the cost and charge of the owner; and if he does not pay the sum so assessed within said four days, then you shall sell at public vendue such distress for payment thereof with charges; first giving forty-eight hours' notice thereof by posting advertisements in some public place in the town" (or plantation, as the case may be;) "and the overplus arising by such sale, if any, beyond the sum assessed and the necessary charges of taking and keeping the distress, you shall immediately restore to the owner; and for want, for twelve days, of goods

and chattels, whereon to make distress, except imple-
ments, tools and articles of furniture exempt from
attachment for debt, you shall take the body of such
person so refusing or neglecting, and him commit to
the jail of the county, there to remain until he pays the
same, or such part thereof, as is not abated by the
assessors for the time being, or the county commissioners for said county

Given under our hands, by virtue of a warrant from
the treasurer aforesaid, this——day of——, 18—.

} Assessors."

And a certificate of the assessment of any state tax
shall be in substance as follows :

"Pursuant to a warrant from the treasurer of the
State of Maine dated the——day of——, 18–, we have
assessed the polls and estates of the——of——, the
sum of——dollars and——cents, and have committed
lists thereof to the——of said——, viz : to—— ——,
with warrants in due form of law for collecting and
paying the same to—— ——, treasurer of state, or his
successor in office, on or before the——day of——,
next ensuing.

In witness whereof, we have hereunto set o r hands
at——, this——day of——, 18—.

} Assessors."

**Form of war-
rant for collec-
tion of county
and town taxes.** SECT. 191.   The warrant for collection of county or
town taxes, shall be made by the assessors in the same
tenor, with proper changes.

**New warrant
issued in case of
loss.** SECT. 192.   When an original warrant issued by
assessors and delivered to a constable or collector for
collection of a tax, has been lost or destroyed by accident, the assessors may issue a new warrant for that
purpose, which shall have the same force as the original.

**Town collectors,
compensation
and appoint-
ment of, in
certain cases.** SECT. 193.   When towns choose collectors, they may
agree what sum shall be allowed for performance of
their duties ; but if none are chosen, or if those chosen
refuse to serve or give the requisite bond, the assessors
may appoint a suitable person to act as constable and
collector for the collection of taxes ; and if the person

so appointed refuses to serve or to give the requisite bond, then they may appoint one of their own board to act as constable and collector for the collection of taxes.

SECT. 194. In case of distress or commitment for non-payment of taxes, the officer shall have the same fees which sheriffs have for levying executions, except that travel, in case of distress, shall be computed only from the dwelling-house of the officer to the place where it is made. *Fees and travel of collector.*

SECT. 195. Every collector or constable, required to collect taxes, shall receive a warrant from the selectmen or assessors of the kind hereinbefore mentioned, and shall faithfully obey its directions. *Collector to receive a warrant.*

SECT. 196. The assessors shall require such constable or collector to give bond for the faithful discharge of his duty, to the inhabitants of the town, in such sum, and with such sureties, as the municipal officers approve ; and bonds of collectors of plantations shall be given to the inhabitants thereof, approved by the assessors, with like conditions. *To give approved bond.*

SECT. 197. When a tax is paid to a collector or constable, he shall give a receipt therefor on demand ; and if he neglects or refuses so to do, he forfeits five dollars to the aggrieved party, to be recovered in an action of debt. *Constables, &c., to give receipts on demand.* *—penalty.*

SECT. 198. If a constable or collector dies before perfecting the collection of an assessment, the assessors shall appoint, at the charge of their town, some suitable person to perfect the collection, and grant him a sufficient warrant for that purpose. *If collector dies, assessors to appoint one.*

SECT. 199. All plantations, required to pay any portion of the public taxes, have all the powers of towns so far as relates to the choice of constables and collectors and the requiring bonds from them. *Plantations may choose collectors.*

SECT. 200. If a person refuses to pay any part of the tax assessed against him in accordance with this chapter, the person whose duty it is to collect the same, may distrain him by any of his goods and chattels not exempt, for the whole or any part of his tax, and may keep such distress for four days at the expense of the owner, and if he does not pay his tax within that time, the distress *Collectors to distrain if taxes are not paid.*

shall be openly sold at vendue by the officer for its pay-

—notice of sale. ment.   Notice of such sale shall be posted in some public place in the town, at least forty-eight hours before the expiration of said four days.

Overplus.   SECT. 201.   The officer, after deducting the tax and expense of sale, shall restore the balance to the former owner, with a written account of the sale and charges.

After twelve days' notice, may imprison.   SECT. 202   If a person so assessed, for twelve days after demand, refuses or neglects to pay his tax and to show the constable or collector sufficient goods and chattels to pay it, such officer may arrest and commit him to jail, until he pays it, or is discharged by law. If the constable or collector has just grounds to fear that any person so assessed may abscond before the

—if about to abscond.   end of said twelve days, he may demand immediate payment, and on refusal, he may commit him as aforesaid.

When payable by instalments, whole may be demanded of one about to remove.   SECT. 203.   When a tax is made payable by instalments, and any person, who was an inhabitant of the town at the time of making such tax, and assessed therein, is about to remove therefrom before the time fixed for any payment, the collector or constable may demand and levy the whole tax, though the time for collecting any instalment has not arrived ; and in default of payment he may distrain for it, or take the course provided in section two hundred and two.

Former collectors to complete collections.   SECT. 204.   When new constables or collectors are chosen and sworn before the former officers have perfected their collections, the latter shall complete the same, as if others had not been chosen and sworn.

Collectors may distrain shares in a corporation.   SECT. 205.   For non-payment of taxes, the collector or constable may distrain the shares owned by the delinquent in the stock of any corporation ; and the same proceedings shall be had as when like property is seized and sold on execution.

Duties of officers of the corporation.   SECT. 206.   The proper officer of such corporation, on request of such constable or collector, shall give him a certificate of the shares or interest owned by the delinquent therein, and issue to the purchaser certificates of such shares according to the by-laws of the corporation.

Collectors may collect in any part of state, of persons removed.   SECT. 207.   When a person taxed in a town in which he was living at the time of assessment, removes therefrom before paying his tax, such constable or collector may demand it of him in any part of the state, and, if he refuses to pay, may distrain him by his goods, and for want thereof may commit him to the jail of the county where he is found, to remain until his tax is paid ; and he shall have the same power to distrain property and arrest the body in any part of the state, as in the place where the tax is assessed.

SECT. 208. Any collector of taxes, or his executor or administrator, may, after due notice, sue in his own name for any tax, in an action of debt, and no trial justice or judge of any municipal or police court before whom such suit is brought, is incompetent to try the same by reason of his residence in the town assessing said tax. Where before suit the person taxed dies or removes to any other town, parish or place in the state, or, being an unmarried woman, marries, the aforesaid notice is not requisite, but the plaintiff shall recover no costs, unless payment was demanded before suit. *(marginal: Collector or administrator may sue for tax. —town magistrate may try case. —when no costs for plaintiff unless demand before suit.)*

SECT. 209. If money not raised for a legal object, is assessed with other moneys legally raised, the assessment is not void ; nor shall any error, mistake or omission by the assessors, collector, or treasurer, render it void ; but any person paying such tax, may bring his action against the town in the supreme judicial court for the same county, and shall recover the sum not raised for a legal object, with twenty five per cent. interest and costs, and any damages which he has sustained by reason of the mistakes, errors, or omissions of such officers. *(marginal: Assessments not void, although they include sums raised for an illegal object. —persons paying illegal tax may recover of town.)*

SECT. 210. When the owner of improved lands living in this state, but not in the town where the estate lies, is taxed, and neglects for six months after the lists of assessment are committed to an officer for collection, to pay his tax, such officer may distrain him by his goods and chattels, and for want thereof may commit him to jail in the county where he is found ; or after two months' written notice, may sue him for such tax in his own name in an action of debt. *(marginal: Collections, how made, of non-residents of improved lands. —may be sued after two months' notice.)*

SECT. 211. When the owner or possessor of goods, wares and merchandise, logs timber, boards and other lumber, stock in trade, including stock employed in the business *(marginal: Collection of taxes on personal property of non-residents.)*

of any of the mechanic arts, horses, mules, neat cattle, sheep or swine, resides in any other town than the one in which such personal property is kept and taxed, the constable or collector having a tax on any such property for collection, may demand it of such owner or possessor in any part of the state, and on his refusal to pay, may distrain him by his goods, and for want thereof, may commit him to jail in the county where he is found, until he pays it or is discharged by law.

Collectors may demand aid.

SECT. 212.   Any collector impeded in collecting taxes, in the execution of his office, may require proper persons to assist him in any town where it is necessary, and any person refusing when so required, shall, on

—penalty for refusing.

complaint, pay not exceeding six dollars at the discretion of the justice before whom the conviction is had, if it appears that such aid was necessary ; and on default of payment, the justice may commit him to jail for forty-eight hours.

Collectors to exhibit account of collections once in two months.

SECT. 213.   Every collector of taxes shall once in two months at least exhibit to the municipal officers, or where there are none, to the assessors of his town, a just and true account of all moneys received on taxes committed to him, and produce the treasurer's receipts for money by him paid ; and for neglect, he forfeits to

—penalty for neglect.

the town two and a half per cent. on the sums committed to him to collect.

Collectors removed or removing, may be required to give up tax bills and settle.

SECT. 214.   When a collector having taxes committed to him to collect, has removed ; or in the judgment of the municipal officers, assessors, or treasurer of a town, or committee or treasurer of a parish, is about to remove from the state before the time set in his warrants to make payment to such treasurer ; or when the time has elapsed, and the treasurer has issued his warrant of distress ; in either case, said officers or committee, may call a meeting of such town or parish, to appoint a committee to settle with him for the money that he has received on his tax bills, to demand and receive of him such bills, and to discharge him therefrom ; said meeting may elect another constable or collector, and the assessors shall make a new warrant

—new warrant to new collector.

and deliver to him with said bills, to collect the sums

due thereon, and he shall have the same power in their collection as the original collector.

SECT. 215.   If such collector or constable refuses to deliver the bills of assessment, and to pay all moneys in his hands collected by him, when duly demanded, he forfeits two hundred dollars to the town or parish, as the case may be, and is liable to pay what remains due on said bills of assessment. *Penalty for refusing to deliver tax bills.*

SECT. 216.   When a constable or collector of taxes dies, becomes insane, has a guardian, or by bodily infirmities is incapable of doing the duties of his office before completing the collection, the assessors may appoint some suitable person a collector to perfect such collection, and may grant him a warrant for the purpose ; and he shall have the same power as the disqualified collector or constable ; but no person shall be so appointed without his consent ; and in these cases, the assessors may demand and receive the tax bills of any person in possession thereof, and deliver them to the new collector. *Collector becoming incapable, another may be appointed.*

SECT. 217.   When it appears that such insane or disqualified constable or collector had paid to the treasurer a larger sum than he had collected from the persons in his list, the assessors in their warrant to such new constable or collector, shall direct him to pay such sum to the guardian of such insane, or to such disqualified constable or collector. *Sums by him overpaid, to be restored.*

SECT. 218.   The treasurer of state shall issue a warrant of distress, signed by him, against any constable or collector to whom a tax has been committed for collection, who is negligent in paying into the public treasury the money required within the time limited by law ; and shall direct it to the sheriff of the county in which such negligent officer lives, or to his deputy returnable in sixty days from its date, to cause the sum due to be levied, with interest from the day fixed for payment, and fifty cents for the warrant, by distress and sale of such deficient officer's real or personal estate, returning any overplus that there may be, and for want thereof, to commit him to jail until he pays it ; and the sheriff shall obey such warrant.   Warrants not satisfied may *Treasurer of state may issue his warrant against delinquent collectors.* *—unsatisfied warrants may be renewed.*

be renewed for the amount unpaid, and shall be of like validity and executed in like manner.

SECT. 219.   When the time for collecting a state tax has expired, and it is unpaid, the treasurer of state shall. at the request of the municipal officers of any town, issue his execution against the collector thereof.

SECT. 220.   If a collector of any town fails to pay the county tax for forty days after the time fixed therefor, the county treasurer shall issue his warrant against him in due form of law, returnable in three months from its date, directed to the sheriff or his deputy, requiring him to collect the tax, with six per cent. interest thereon from the time it was payable, fifty cents for the warrant, and his own legal fees.

SECT. 221.   If a deficient constable or collector has no estate which can be distrained, and his person cannot be found within three months after a warrant of distress issues from the treasurer of state, or, if being committed to jail, he does not within three months satisfy it, his town shall, within three months more, pay to the state the sums due from him.

SECT. 222.   The assessors having written notice from such treasurer of the failure of their constable or collector, shall forthwith, without any further warrant, assess the sum so due upon the inhabitants of their town as the sum so committed was assessed, and commit it to another constable or collector for collection; and if they neglect. the state treasurer shall issue his warrant against them for the whole sum due from such constable or collector, which shall be executed by the sheriff or his deputy, as other warrants issued by such treasurer.   If after such second assessment, the tax is not paid to the treasurer within three months from the date of its commitment, the treasurer may issue his warrant to the sheriff of the county requiring him to levy it on real and personal property of any inhabitants of the town, as hereinbefore provided.

SECT. 223.   Such deficient collector or constable shall at all times be answerable to such inhabitants for all sums which they have been obliged to pay by means of his deficiency, and for all consequent damages.

SECT. 224. If a collector or constable of a town or parish dies without settling his accounts of taxes committed to him to collect, his executor or administrator, within two months after his acceptance of the trust, shall settle with such assessors for what was received by the deceased in his life time; with the amount so received, such executor or administrator is chargeable as the deceased would be if living; and if he fails so to settle, when he has sufficient assets in his hands, he shall be chargeable with the whole sum committed to the deceased for collection. *(When collector dies, administrator to settle within two months; failing to do so, chargeable with amount.)*

SECT. 225. If the constable or collector of any town or parish, to whom taxes have been committed for collection, neglects to collect and pay them to the treasurer named in the warrant of the assessors by the time therein stated, such treasurer shall issue his warrant, returnable in ninety days, and in substance as follows, to the sheriff of the county or his deputy, who shall execute it. *(Treasurer to issue his warrant against delinquent collectors.)*

"A. B.. treasurer of the——of——, in the county of ——, to the sheriff of said county, or his deputy, *(—form of warrant.)*

GREETING.

Whereas C. D., of   aforesaid, (addition) on the   day of   , 18 , being a   of taxes granted and agreed on by the   aforesaid, had a list of assessments duly made by the assessors of the   aforesaid, amounting to the sum of $.   , committed to him with a warrant under their hands, directing and empowering him to collect the several sums in said assessment mentioned, and pay the same to the treasurer of the   aforesaid by the   day of   , 18 , but the said C. D. has been remiss in his duty by law required, and has neglected to collect the several sums aforesaid, and pay them to the treasurer of the   aforesaid; and there still remains due thereof the sum of $.   , and the said C D still neglects to pay it: You are hereby, in the name of the State, required forthwith to levy the aforesaid sum of $.   , by distress and sale of the estate, real or personal, of said C. D., and pay the same to the treasurer of said   , returning the overplus, if any, to said C. D. And for want of such estate, to take the body of said C. D., and him

commit to the jail in the county aforesaid, there to remain until he has paid the said sum of $.   ,
with forty cents for this warrant, together with your fees, or he is otherwise discharged therefrom by order of law ; and make return of this warrant to myself, or my successor, as treasurer of said   , within ninety days from this time, with your doings therein.

Given under my hand, this   day of   , in the year eighteen hundred and   .

, Treasurer of   ."

Sheriff's duty respecting such warrant.
SECT. 226. On each execution or warrant of distress issued by the treasurer of state, or by the treasurer of a county, town, or parish, against a constable or collector, and delivered to a sheriff or his deputy, he shall make return of his doings to such treasurer. within a reasonable time after the return day therein mentioned, with the money, if any, that he has received by virtue thereof ; and if he neglects to comply with any direction of such warrant or execution, he shall pay the whole sum mentioned therein. When it is returned unsatisfied, or satisfied in part only, such treasurer may issue an alias for the sum due on the return of the first ; and so on. as often as occasion occurs. A reasonable time after the return day, shall be computed at the rate of forty-eight hours for every ten miles distance from the dwelling-house of the sheriff or his deputy to the place where the warrant is returnable.

—treasurer may issue an alias warrant.

Warrants to be issued to coroner, when sheriff is delinquent.
SECT. 227. When a sheriff or deputy is deficient as aforesaid, such treasurers may direct warrants to a coroner of the county, requiring him to distrain therefor upon the delinquent's real or personal estate ; and the coroner shall execute such warrants as a sheriff does on deficient constables and collectors.

Property distrained to be sold as on execution.
SECT. 228. Any officer selling personal property distrained under a warrant from such treasurers against a deficient constable or collector, shall proceed as in the sale of such property on execution.

Real estate taken, how notified to be sold.
SECT. 229. When a warrant of distress from such treasurers is levied on the real estate of a deficient constable, collector, sheriff, or deputy sheriff, for the purpose of sale, fourteen days' notice of the sale, and of

the time and place, shall be given, by posting advertisements in two or more public places in the town or
place where the estate lies, and in two adjoining towns.

SECT. 230. At that time and place, the officer hav- Proceedings at sale.
ing such warrant shall sell, at public vendue, so much
of such estate, in common and undivided with the residue, if any, as is necessary to satisfy the sum named
in the warrant, with all legal charges; and execute to —deed made to
the purchaser a sufficient deed thereof, which shall be convey title.
as effectual as if executed by the deficient owner.

SECT. 231. If the proceeds of such sale do not Proceedings when body is
satisfy such sum and legal charges, the treasurer who taken.
issued the warrant, shall issue an alias warrant for the
sum remaining due; and the officer executing it shall
arrest such deficient officer, and proceed as on an
execution for debt; and such deficient officer shall have
the same rights and privileges as a debtor arrested or
committed on execution in favor of a private creditor.

SECT. 232. When any constable or collector of taxes —rights and privileges of
is taken on execution under this chapter, the assessors party arrested.
may demand of him a true copy of the assessments,
which he received of them and then has in his hands
unsettled, with the evidence of all payments made
thereon; and if he complies with this demand, he shall
receive such credit as the assessors, on inspection of
the assessment, adjudge him entitled to, and account
for the balance; but if he refuses, he shall forthwith be
committed to jail by the officer who so took him, or by
a warrant from a justice of the peace, to remain there
until he complies; and the assessors shall take and use
copies of the record of assessments instead of the
copies demanded of him.

SECT. 233. The same town or parish may, at any When dis-
time. proceed to the choice of another collector, to charged from arrest, town
complete the collection of the assessments, who shall liable for state and county
be sworn and give the security required of the first taxes.
collector; and the assessors shall deliver to him the
uncollected assessments, with a proper warrant for
their collection, and he shall proceed as before prescribed.

11

Collector liable for tax, unless he commits within a year.

Sect. 234. When the tax of any person named in said assessment does not thereby appear to have been paid, but such person declares that it was paid to the former collector, the new collector shall not distrain or commit him, without a vote of such town or parish first certified to him by its clerk.

Fees for commitment.

Municipal officers may direct suit for taxes to be commenced against any delinquent.

—proviso.

Sect. 235. When a town neglects to choose any constable or collector to collect a state or county tax, the sheriff of the county shall collect it, on receiving an assessment thereof, with a warrant under the hands of the assessors of such town, duly chosen, or appointed by the county commissioners, as the case may be.

Towns may appoint treasurer collector, his assistants to give bond.

Sect. 236. When plantations neglect to choose constables or collectors, or if those chosen and accepting their trust neglect their duty, such plantations shall be proceeded against as in the case of deficient towns : and such deficient constables or collectors are liable to the same penalties, and shall be removed in the same manner, as deficient constables and collectors of towns.

Abatement for voluntary payment of taxes.

Sect. 237. The sheriff or his deputy, on receiving such assessment and warrant for collection as is mentioned in the two preceding sections, shall forthwith post in some public place in the town or plantation assessed, an attested copy of such assessment and warrant, and shall make no distress for any of such taxes until after thirty days therefrom ; and any person paying his tax to such sheriff within that time, shall pay five per cent.

—notice shall be posted.

over and above his tax for sheriff's fees, and no more ; but those who do not pay within that time shall be distrained or arrested by such officer, as by collectors ; and the sheriff may require aid for the purpose, and the same fees shall be paid for travel and service of the sheriff, as in other cases of distress.

Proceedings, when body is taken.

Sect. 238. When an officer appointed to collect assessments by virtue of a warrant, for want of property arrests any person and commits him to jail, he shall give an attested copy of his warrant to the jailer, and certify, under his hand, the sum that he is to pay as his tax and the costs of arresting and committing. and that for want of goods and chattels whereon to make distress, he has arrested him ; and such copy and certificate are a sufficient warrant to require the jailer to receive and —rights and privileges of party arrested. keep such person in custody, until he pays his tax, charges, and thirty-three cents for the copy of the warrant; but he shall have the rights and privileges, mentioned in section one hundred and sixty-four.

SECT. 239. When a person, committed for non-payment of taxes due to the state or county, is discharged by virtue of any statute for the relief of poor prisoners confined in jail for taxes, the town whose assessors issued the warrant by which he was committed shall pay the whole tax required of it

When discharged from arrest, town liable for state and county taxes.

SECT. 240. When a person imprisoned for not paying his tax, is discharged, the officer committing him shall not be discharged from such tax without a vote of the town, unless he imprisoned him within one year after the taxes were committed to him to collect.

Collector liable for tax, unless he commits within a year.

SECT. 241. For commitments for non-payment of taxes, the officer shall have the same fees as for levying executions, but his travel shall be computed only from his dwelling-house to the place of commitment.

Fees for commitment.

SECT. 242. In addition to the other provisions for the collection of taxes legally assessed, the mayor and treasurer of any city, the selectmen of any town, and the assessors of any plantation to which a tax is due, may in writing direct an action of debt to be commenced in the name of such city or of the inhabitants of such town or plantation, against the party liable; but no such defendant is liable for any costs of suit, unless it appears by the declaration and by proof, that payment of said tax had been duly demanded before said suit.

Municipal officers may direct suit for taxes to be commenced against any delinquent.

—proviso.

SECT. 243 In all suits to collect a tax on real estate, if it appears that at the date of the list on which such tax was made the record title to the real estate listed was in the defendant, he shall not deny his title thereto; provided, however, if any owner of real estate who has conveyed the same shall forthwith file a copy of the description as given in his deed, with the date thereof and the name and residence of his grantee, in the registry of deeds where such deed should be recorded, he shall be free from any liability under this act. When such suits are commenced within eighteen months from

In suits to collect tax on real estate, if record title appears to be in defendant, he shall not deny his title thereto.

—proviso.

—when judgment shall be lien on land.

the date of the list, after such notice to the owners as
the court shall order, the judgment recovered against
the defendant therein shall be a lien on the land relating
back to the date of the list and continuing for thirty
days after rendition of judgment, to be enforced on
execution in any of the methods now provided by law.

Duties of Town Treasurers, when Appointed Collectors of Taxes.

Towns may appoint treasurer collector, his assistants to give bond.

SECT. 244.   The inhabitants of a town may in March
annually appoint their treasurer a collector of taxes ;
and he may then appoint under him such number of
assistants as are necessary, who shall give bond for the
faithful discharge of their duties in such sum and with
such sureties, as the municipal officers approve ; and he
shall have such powers as are vested in collectors chosen for that purpose

Abatement for voluntary payment of taxes.

SECT. 245.   At any meeting, when it votes to raise
a tax, a town may agree on the abatement to be made
to those who voluntarily pay their taxes to the collector or treasurer at certain periods, and the times within
which they are so entitled ; and a notification of such
votes, and the time when such taxes must be paid to

—notice shall be posted.

obtain the abatement, shall be posted by the treasurer
in one or more public places in his town, within seven
days after such commitment ; and all who so pay their

—abatement not to exceed ten per cent. of tax.

taxes are entitled to such abatement ; but no person
shall receive an abatement of more than ten per cent.
of his tax ; and all taxes not so paid shall be collected
by the collector or his deputy, under the other provisions of this chapter.

Assessors to deposit assessment with treasurer.

SECT. 246.   The assessors of any town which at its
annual meeting regulates the collection of its taxes
agreeably to the two preceding sections, shall assess the
same in due form, and deposit them in the hands of the
treasurer for collection, with their warrant for that purpose, after he and his deputies are qualified.

Treasurers' powers continue until collection is completed.

SECT 247.   All the powers granted in this chapter to
treasurers, who are appointed collectors of taxes, are
extended until the collection of any tax committed to

them has been completed, notwithstanding the year for which they were appointed has elapsed.

Sect. 248. The municipal officers of towns shall require the treasurer thereof to give bond, with sufficient sureties, for faithful performance of the duties of his office, and if he negl cts or refuses, it shall be deemed a refusal to accept the office, and the town shall proceed to a new choice, as in case of vacancy. *Treasurer to give bond.*

Sect. 249. Every treasurer shall render an account of the finances of his town, and exhibit all books and accounts pertaining to his office, to the municipal officers thereof, or to any c mmittee appointed by it to examine said accounts. when required ; and such officers shall examine such treasurer's accounts as often as once in three months. *To render account once in three months.*

Sect. 250. The treasurer of any town who is also a collector, may issue his warrant to the sheriff of any county or to his deputy, or to a constable of his town, directing him to distrain the person or property of any person delinquent in paying his taxes, after the expiration of the time fixed for payment by vote of the town ; which warrant shall be of the same tenor as that prescribed to be issued by municipal officers or assessors to collectors, with the appropriate changes, returnable to the treasurer in thirty, sixty or ninety days. *Treasurer of town who is collector may issue warrant to sheriff to collect taxes.* *—form of warrant.* *—when returnable.*

Sect. 251. When such treasurer thinks that there is danger of losing by delay a tax assessed on any individual, he may distrain his person or property before the expiration of the time fixed by vote of the town. *May distrain before tax is due, to prevent loss.*

Sect. 252. Before such officer serves any such warrant, he shall deliver to the delinquent, or leave at his last and usual place of abode, a summons from said collector and treasurer, stating the amount of tax due, and that it must be paid within ten days from the time of leaving such summons, with twenty cents for the officer for leaving the same ; and if not so paid, the officer shall serve such warrant the same as collectors of taxes may do. and shall receive the same fees as for levying executions in personal actions. *Ten days' notice before distraining.* *—powers and fees of officer, same as collectors'.*

Special Provisions.

Affidavit of person posting notices of land sales, evidence.

SECT. 253. The affidavit of any disinterested person as to posting notifications required for the sale of any land to be sold by the sheriff or his deputy, constable or collector, in the execution of his office, may be used in evidence in any trial to prove the fact of notice ; if such affidavit, made on one of the original advertisements, or on a copy of it, is filed in the registry of the county or district where the land lies, within six months.

Owners of estate taken for default of others, may recover its value.

SECT. 254   When the estate of an inhabitant of a town or parish, who is not an assessor thereof, is levied upon and taken as mentioned in section one hundred and eleven, he may maintain an action against such town or parish, and recover the full value of the estate so levied on, with interest at the rate of twenty per cent. from the time it was taken, with costs ; and such value may be proved by any other legal evidence, as well as by the result of the sale under such levy.

—value not determined by sale.

Warrants returnable in three months, and may be renewed.

SECT. 255. All warrants lawfully issued by a state or county treasurer, shall be made returnable in three months, and may be renewed for the collection of what appears due upon them when returned, including expenses incurred in attempting to collect them ; and the power and duty of the sheriff shall be the same in executing such alias or pluries warrant, as if it were the original.

—sheriff may execute alias warrant.

Enforced Collection of Taxes on Real Estate.

Lien on lands created by tax.

SECT. 256. For all taxes legally assessed on real estate and on equitable interests assessed under section three, a lien is created which may be enforced by attachment in suit authorized as provided in sections two hundred and eight and two hundred and ten or two hundred and forty-two to be made within two years from date of the original commitment, or by sale in the manner and within the time hereinafter provided.

—how enforced.

—land may be sold.

Collectors' Notice of Sale.

SECT. 257. If any such tax remains unpaid for nine *Proceeding in case of sale.*
months from the date of the commitment the collector
may give notice thereof, and of his intention to sell so
much of such real estate or interest as is necessary for *—notices, how given.*
the payment of said tax and all the charges, by posting
notices thereof in the same manner and at the same places
that warrants for town meetings are therein required to
be posted, six weeks before the day of sale, designating *—what notice must contain.*
the name of the owner, if known, the right, lot, and
range, the number of acres as nearly as may be, the
amount of tax due, and such other short description
taken from the inventory as is necessary to render its
identification certain and plain, with the valuation
thereof, and shall cause said notice to be published in *—notice must be published in newspaper if any in the county.*
some newspaper, if any, published in the county where
such real estate lies, three weeks successively ; such
publication to begin six weeks before the day of sale ;
if no newspaper is published in said county, said notice
shall be published in like manner in the state paper ; *—or in state paper.*
he shall in the notices and advertisements so posted and
published, state the name of the town, and if within
three years it has changed, for the whole or a part of
the territory, both the present and former name shall *—further particulars to be stated in the notices.*
be stated, and that if the taxes, interest and charges
are not paid within eighteen months from the date of
commitment, so much of the estate as is sufficient to
pay the amount due therefor, with interest and charges,
will be sold without further notice, at public auction, at
a place, day and hour therein named, after the expiration of the eighteen months and not exceeding twenty
months from the date of commitment. The date of
commitment, the name of the collector, and notice that
nine months have elapsed since the date of the commitment of said tax to the collector, shall be stated in the
advertisement. Said collector shall lodge with the town *—copy of notice to be filed in town clerk's office, with collector's certificate.*
clerk a copy of such notice, with his certificate thereon
that he has given notice of the intended sale as required
by law. Such copy and certificate shall be recorded by
said clerk and the record so made shall be open to the
inspection of all persons interested. The clerk shall *—clerk must record the copy.*

furnish to any person desiring it an attested copy of such record, on receiving payment or tender of payment of a reasonable sum therefor; but notices of sales of real estate within any village corporation for unpaid taxes of said corporation may be given by notices thereof posted in the same manner and at the same places as warrants for corporation meetings and by publication as aforesaid.

Form.

SECT. 258.   The notice and advertisement of the collector shall be in substance as follows:

"Unpaid taxes on lands of resident and non-resident owners, situated in the town of   , in the County of   , in the year .

(N. B.)   The name of the town was formerly   (to be stated in case of change of name, as mentioned in section 257). · "The following list of taxes on real estate of resident and non-resident owners in the town of   , for the year   , committed to me for collection for said town, on the   day of   , 18 , more than nine months since, remain unpaid; and notice is hereby given that if said taxes, interest and charges are not paid within eighteen months from the date of commitment of said bills, so much of the real estate taxed as is sufficient to pay the amount due therefor, including interest and charges. will be sold at public auction at   , in said town, on the day of   , 18 , at   o'clock M."   (N. B.   Here follows the list. a short description of each parcel taken from the inventory to be inserted in an additional column.)

                        C. D., Collector of Taxes, of the town of   ."

Special Notices to Owners.

SECT. 259. After the land is so advertised, and at least ten days before the day of sale, the collector shall notify the owner if resident, or occupant thereof, if any, of the time and place of sale by delivering to him in person, or leaving at his last and usual place of abode, a copy of such notice signed by him, stating the time and place of sale and the amount of taxes due. In case of non-resident owners of unoccupied lands notice shall be sent by mail to the last and usual address, if known to the collector. ten days before the day of sale. *Owner of advertised lands to be notified specially by the collector.*

—non-residents to be notified by mail.

SECT. 260. When no person appears to discharge the taxes duly assessed on any real estate so advertised, with costs of advertising, on or before the time of sale, the collector shall proceed to sell at public auction to the highest bidder so much of such real estate or interest as is necessary to pay the tax due, with five dollars for advertising and selling it, and twenty-five cents more for each copy required to be lodged with the town clerk, and sixty-seven cents for the deed thereof. and certificate of acknowledgment. If the bidding is for less than the whole, it shall be for a fractional part of the estate, and the bidder who will pay the sum due for the least fractional part shall be the purchaser. If more than one right, lot or parcel of land is so advertised and sold, said charge of five dollars shall be divided equally among the several rights, lots or parcels advertised and sold at any one time ; and the collector shall receive in addition, fifty cents on each parcel of real estate so advertised and sold, when more than one parcel is advertised and sold. *Proceedings at sale.*

—costs specified.

—bidding may be for fractional part of the delinquent land.

—fees divided when more than one lot is sold.

Collector's Return of Sale.

SECT. 261. The collector making any sale of real estate for non-payment of taxes, shall, within thirty days after such sale make a return, with a particular statement of his doings in making such sale, to the clerk of his town ; who shall record it in the town records ; and said return, or if lost or destroyed, an attested copy of the record thereof, shall be evidence of the facts therein set forth in all cases where such collector is not personally interested. *Collector's return of sale to the town clerk.*

—clerk must record the return.

—record, or, if lost, a copy, is evidence when.

Form.

SECT. 262.   The collector's return to the town clerk shall be in substance as follows :

"Pursuant to law I caused the taxes assessed on the real estate described herein, situated in the town of   , for the year   , to be advertised according to law by posting notices as required by law and by advertising in the   three weeks successively the first publication being on the   day of   and at least six weeks before the day of sale ; I also, at least ten days before the day of sale, notified the owners or occupants of said lands, and addressed to the non-resident owners of unoccupied lands whose addresses were known to me, notice of the time and place of said sale in the manner provided by law ; and afterwards on the   day of   , 18   , at   , in said   , at o'clock,   M., being the time and place of sale, I proceeded to sell according to the tenor of the advertisement, the estates upon which the taxes so assessed remained unpaid ; and in the schedule following is set forth each parcel of the estate so offered for sale, the amount of taxes, and the name of the purchaser ; and I have made and executed deeds of the several parcels to the several persons entitled thereto, and placed them on file in the town treasurer's office, to be disposed of as the law requires.

SCHEDULE NO. I.

Name of owner.	Description of property.	Amount of tax. interest and charges.	Quantity sold.	Name of purchaser.

In witness of all which I have hereunto subscribed my name, this ——— day of ———, 18—.
                              C. D., Collector of taxes of the
town of   ."

For his fidelity in discharging the duties herein required, the town is responsible, and has a remedy on his bond in case of default.   He may, if necessary to complete the sale, adjourn the auction from day to day.

Collector's Certificate.

SECT. 263.   When real estate is so sold for taxes, The collector's certificate of the collector shall, within four days after the day of sale; what it must contain; it sale, lodge with the treasurer of his town a certificate must be lodged in treasurer's under oath designating the quantity of land sold, the office with the deed of land names of the owners of each parcel, and the names of sold. the purchasers; what part of the amount of each was tax, and what was cost and charges; also a deed containing a description of each parcel sold, running to the purchasers.

SECT. 264.   The treasurer shall not deliver the deeds Deed not to be delivered until to the grantees but put them on file in his office, to be one year after. delivered at the expiration of one year from the day of sale, in case the owner does not within that time redeem his estate from the sale, by payment of the taxes, interest at the rate aforesaid to the time of redemption, and costs as above provided, with sixty-seven cents for the deed and certificate of acknowledgment. If the deed is recorded within twenty-five months after the —record of deed. day of sale, no intervening attachment or conveyance shall affect the title.

Redemption Within Two Years

SECT. 265.   Any person, to whom the right by law Proprietor may redeem within belongs, may, at any time within two years after such two years. certificate is lodged with the town treasurer, redeem any real estate or interest of resident or non-resident proprietors sold for taxes, on paying into the town treasury for the purchaser, the full amount so certified to be due, both taxes and costs, including the sum allowed for the deeds, with interest on the whole at the rate of twenty per cent. a year from the date of said —money to be received by certificate, which shall be received and held by said treasurer as property of pur- treasurer as the property of the purchaser aforesaid; chaser. and the treasurer shall pay it to said purchaser, his heirs, or assigns, on demand; and if not paid when demanded, the purchaser may recover it in any court of competent jurisdiction, with costs and interest at the ate of twenty per cent. after such demand. The sureties of the treasurer shall pay the same on failure of said treasurer. And in default of payment by either, the town or plantation shall pay the same with costs and interest as aforesaid.

SECT. 266. If no person having legal authority so to do redeems the same within the time aforesaid by paying the full amount required by this chapter, said treasurer shall deliver to the purchaser the deeds so lodged with him by the collector; and if he wilfully refuses to deliver such deed to such purchaser, on

demand, after said two years and forfeiture of the land as aforesaid, he forfeits to said purchaser the full value of the property so to be conveyed, to be recovered in an action of debt, with costs and interest as in other cases; the sureties of said treasurer shall make good the payment here required, in default of payment by the principal; and on the failure of both, the town is liable.

Within What Time Sales Must be Made.

SECT. 267. No sale of real estate for non-payment of taxes under this chapter shall be made by any officer to whom a warrant for their collection has been committed after two years from the date of the original commitment of such taxes, provided that this section

shall not be construed to apply to sales on executions, on attachments to enforce tax liens.

SECT. 268. The copy of the notice of sale and the certificates thereon, deposited with the town clerk, as required in section one hundred and ninety-three, or if they are lost or destroyed, an attested transcript of the town clerk's record thereof; shall be conclusive evidence that such notice was given as is required by this chapter in the trial of all issues, in which the collector who made the sale is not personally interested.

SECT 269. The treasurer's receipt or certificate of payment of a sufficient sum to redeem any lands taxed as aforesaid, shall be legal evidence of such payment and redemption.

Additional Provisions.

SECT. 270.   The municipal officers may employ one of their own number, or some other person, to attend the sale for taxes of any real estate, in which their town is interested, and bid therefor a sum sufficient to pay the amount due and charges, in behalf of the town, and the deed shall be made to it.

Estate may be bid off for town.

SECT. 271.   In all cases where real estate has been sold for state, county or town taxes, the owner may, within the time allowed by law, pay the sums necessary to redeem the same, into the treasury of the state, county or town to which the tax is to be paid, and such payment seasonably made shall redeem the estate. The treasurer shall pay the amount so received by him to the person entitled thereto according to the records and documents in his office.

Owner may redeem; amount received to be paid to person entitled.

SECT. 272.   In the trial of any action at law or in equity involving the validity of any sale of real estate for non-payment of taxes effected since March three, eighteen hundred and seventy-four, it shall be sufficient for the party claiming under it, in the first instance, to produce in evidence the collector's or treasurer's deed, duly executed and recorded, and then he shall be entitled to judgment in his favor unless the party contesting such sale, or the person under whom he claims, shall have deposited with the clerk of the court in which such action is pending, before the beginning of his said action or defence the amount of all such taxes, interest and costs accruing under such sale, and of all taxes paid after such sale, and interest thereon, to be paid out by order of court to the party legally and equitably entitled thereto, and then he may be admitted to prosecute or defend ; but if the other party then produces in addition to the deed as aforesaid the assessments signed by the assessors and their warrant to the collector, and proves that such collector or treasurer complied with the requirements of law in advertising and selling such real estate, he shall have judgment in his favor ; and in all such actions involving the validity of sales made after this act takes effect, the collector's

Validity of sale of real estate for taxes.

—treasurer's deed and assessments, evidence.

—contestant's suit not maintainable until taxes and charges are paid into court.

—when the other party may have judgment.

—return and
record or copy,
when conclu-
sive evidence of
facts alleged
therein.
return to the town clerk, the town clerk's record, or if lost or destroyed, said clerk's attested copy of such record as provided in section two hundred and sixty-one, shall be conclusive evidence of all facts therein alleged.

But not to re-
lieve from neg-
ligence of
collector.
SECT. 273.   The foregoing section shall not be construed to relieve any collector from liability for damages occasioned to any party by his negligence or misfeasance as such collector.

In suits to col-
lect tax on real
estate, if record
title appears to
be in defendant,
he shall not
deny his title
thereto.

—proviso.
SECT. 274.   In all suits to collect a tax on real estate, if it appears that at the date of the list on which such tax was made the record title to the real estate listed was in the defendant, he shall not deny his title thereto ; provided, however, if any owner of real estate who has conveyed the same shall forthwith file a copy of the description as given in his deed, with the date thereof and the name and residence of his grantee, in the registry of deeds where such deed should be recorded, he shall be free from any liability under this act.   —when judgment shall be
lien on land. When such suits are commenced within eighteen months from the date of the list, after such notice to the owners as the court shall order, the judgment recovered against the defendant therein shall be a lien on the land relating back to the date of the list and continuing for thirty days after rendition of judgment, to be enforced on execution in any of the methods now provided by law.

An Act to amend sections seventy-nine, eighty-two and eighty-three of Chapter Three of the Revised Statutes.

Sections seventy-nine, eighty-two and eighty-three of chapter three of the Revised Statutes are amended by striking out the words "state treasurer" and "treasurer of state" wherever they occur in said sections and by inserting instead thereof in each instance the words "state assessors;" and by striking out the last word in section seventy-nine and inserting the word "them" instead thereof, so that said sections as amended shall read as follows:

"SECT. 79. The assessors first chosen in plantations organized under section seventy-one, shall immediately take an inventory of the polls and valuation of the property therein, as the same as taken in towns, and return them on or before the fifteenth day of May following their election, to the county commissioners of their county, who may examine and correct the same so as to make it conform to the last state valuation, and return a copy of such corrected valuation to the state assessors, and thereupon their ratable proportion according to such valuation, of all state and county taxes, shall be assessed on such plantations in the same manner as on towns; and such plantations, and also such as may by special order of the legislature be required to pay state or county taxes, may raise money by taxation for making and repairing ways in compliance with chapter eighteen, sections thirty-nine and ninety-seven. Such inventory and valuation in any plantation shall be so taken, corrected and returned to the state assessors whenever required by them."

"SECT. 82. When towns are incorporated, the assessors thereof shall return to the county commissioners of their county the original valuation first taken in their towns, on or before the fifteenth day of May next following their incorporation, and said valuation shall be examined, corrected, and a copy thereof returned to the state assessors, to become the basis of state and county taxes in the same manner as the valuation of plantations, as provided in section seventy-nine."

"SECT. 83. If such valuation is not made and returned by any town or plantation within the time specified, the county commissioners shall appoint three suitable persons of the county to be assessors therein, who shall be sworn and make and return the inventory and valuation required, within the time fixed by said commissioners ; and such valuation shall be examined, corrected, and a copy thereof returned to the state assessors, and become a basis for the assessment of state and county taxes, in the same manner as if the valuation had been taken by the assessors chosen by said town or plantation."

An Act to amend sections twelve and thirty-two of Chapter Three of the Revised Statutes.

SECT. 1.   Section twelve of chapter three of the Revised Statutes is amended by adding to said section the words following : "Towns having less than two thousand inhabitants, by the last preceding census, may choose three or more assessors or the selectmen may be assessors as provided by section one hundred and seventy of chapter six ; but towns having more than two thousand inhabitants, by such census, shall choose three or five assessors as follows : At the annual town meeting next held after this act becomes operative, if such town shall elect *three* assessors it shall elect one of them to serve for one year, one for two years and one for three years and one at each annual meeting thereafter to serve for three years ; if such town shall elect *five* assessors, two of them shall be elected for one year, two for two years and one for three years, and thereafter, at each annual meeting, shall elect one or two for three years as their terms shall expire.   In towns having more than two thousand inhabitants, as aforesaid, the selectmen shall not be assessors," so that said section, as amended, shall read as follows :

"SECT. 12.   Annual town meetings shall be held in March, and the voters shall then choose, by a majority vote, a clerk, three, five or seven inhabitants of the town to be selectmen and overseers of the poor, when other overseers are not chosen, three or more assessors, two or more fence viewers, treasurer, surveyors of lumber, tythingmen, sealers of leather, measurers of wood and bark, constables, collectors of taxes, and other usual town officers ; and if one-third of the voters present are in favor thereof, they shall choose, by major vote, one auditor of accounts, all of whom shall be sworn. Treasurers or collectors of towns having more than fifteen hundred inhabitants shall not be selectmen or assessors. Towns having less than two thousand inhabitants, by the last preceding census, may choose three or more assessors or the selectmen may be assessors as provided by section one hundred and two of chapter six, but towns having more than two thousand inhabitants, by such census, shall choose three or five assessors as follows : At the annual town meeting next held after this act becomes operative, if such town shall elect *three* assessors it shall elect one of them to serve for one year, one for two years and one for three years and one at each annual meeting thereafter to serve for three years ; if such town shall elect five assessors, two of them shall be elected for one year, two for two years and one for three years, and thereafter, at each annual meeting, shall elect one or two for three years as their terms shall expire. In towns having more than two thousand inhabitants, as aforesaid, the selectmen shall not be assessors."

SECT. 2. Section thirty-two of said chapter is amended by striking out the words "assessors and" in the first line and by adding to said section the words following : "And, unless otherwise provided in their charters, assessors shall be chosen on said day to hold office as provided for the election of assessors in towns having more than two thousand inhabitants by section twelve ;" so that said section, as amended, shall read as follows :

SECT. 32. "The subordinate officers of cities, when their charters do not otherwise provide, shall be chosen on the second Monday of March, annually, or as soon after as practicable, and hold their offices one year therefrom, and until others are chosen and qualified in their stead, and, unless otherwise provided in their charters, assessors shall be chosen on said day to hold office as provided for the election of assessors in towns having more than two thousand inhabitants by section twelve."

12

An Act to amend section seventy-three of Chapter Forty-Nine of the Revised Statutes.

Section seventy-three of chapter forty-nine of the Revised Statutes is hereby amended by striking out the word "one" in the ninth line and inserting instead thereof the word "two", so that said section, as amended, shall read as follows :

SECT. 73. "No person shall act as agent of an insurance company until he has filed with the commissioner a duplicate power of attorney from the company or its authorized agent empowering him to so act. Upon filing such power the commissioner shall issue a license to him if the company is a domestic company or has received a license to do business in this state ; and such license shall continue until the first day of the next July, and may be renewed from year to year on producing a certificate from the company that his agency is continued. For each such license or renewal the commissioner shall receive two dollars. And if any person solicits, receives or forwards any risk or application for insurance to any company, without first receiving such license, or fraudulently assumes to be an agent, and thus procures risks and receives money for premiums he forfeits not more than fifty dollars for each offence ; but any policy issued on such application, binds the company, if otherwise valid.

An Act to repeal certain acts consolidated in "An Act to provide for the raising of Revenue by Taxation.

SECT. 1. The following public acts or sections of acts, named and herein designated are repealed except so far as they are preserved in the following section :

Chapter six of the Revised Statutes, entitled "The assessment and collection of taxes."

Chapter three hundred and twenty-nine of the Public Laws of 1885, entitled "An Act providing for the taxation of life insurance companies.

Section two of chapter three hundred and fifty-nine of the Public Laws of 1885, entitled "An Act to amend the Revised Statutes."

Chapter three hundred and fifty-three of the Public Laws of 1885, entitled "An Act to amend section seventy of chapter six of the Revised Statutes, relating to assessment of taxes in places not incorporated."

Chapter three hundred and fifty of the Public Laws of 1885, entitled "An Act to amend section one hundred and seventy-five of chapter six of the Revised Statutes, relating to suit for taxes."

Chapter seventy-five of the Public Laws of 1887, entitled "An Act to amend section forty-one of chapter six of the Revised Statutes, relating to tax on railroads."

Chapter seventy-two of the Public Laws of 1887, entitled "An Act additional to and amendatory of sections fifty-five, fifty-six, fifty-seven and fifty-eight of chapter six of the Revised Statutes, relating to corporations."

Chapter seventy-four of the Public Laws of 1887, entitled "An Act to amend section sixty-four of chapter six of the Revised Statutes, relating to taxation of corporations."

Chapter eighty of the Public Laws of 1887, entitled "An Act additional to and amendatory of section eighty-two of chapter six of the Revised Statutes, relating to the collection of highway taxes on lands in unincorporated places."

Chapter two hundred and ninety-six of the Public Laws of 1889, entitled "An Act in relation to suits for taxes."

Chapter one hundred and seventy-five of the Public Laws of 1889, entitled "An Act in relation to the taxation of trust funds."

Chapter two hundred and seventy-four of the Public Laws of 1889, entitled "An Act to amend section six, chapter six of the Revised Statutes, relative to property exempt from taxation."

SECT. 2. The acts declared to be repealed remain in force for the trial and punishment of all past violations of them, and for the recovery of penalties and forfeitures already incurred and for the preservation of all rights and their remedies existing by virtue of them, and so far as they apply to any office, trust, judicial proceeding, right, contract, limitation or event already affected by them. The repeal of the acts aforesaid does not revive any of the acts repealed by them.

APPENDIX.

Table I—Comparative State Valuations.

COUNTIES.	STATE VALUATION 1880.				STATE VALUATION 1890 AS RETURNED BY ASSESSORS.			Increase.	Decrease.
	Polls.	Estates.	Wild lands.	Total.	Real.	Personal.	Aggregate.		
Androscoggin	10,312	$20,776,973	—	$20,776,973	$18,569,779	3,778,317	$22,348,096	$1,571,123	
Aroostook	7,734	6,225,834	$2,339,098	7,564,932	6,292,205	2,255,172	8,547,377	982,445	
Cumberland	21,539	51,530,510	—	51,530,510	41,458,889	17,843,058	59,301,947	7,771,437	
Franklin	4,791	5,812,866	340,746	6,153,612	4,203,514	1,410,822	5,614,336	—	539,276
Hancock	9,660	7,897,488	377,478	8,274,966	11,366,494	2,593,480	13,959,971	5,685,008	
Kennebec	13,252	23,292,164	—	23,292,164	18,622,728	6,148,140	24,770,928	1,478,764	
Knox	9,087	10,878,736	—	10,878,736	8,096,011	3,619,193	11,715,204	836,468	
Lincoln	6,750	6,634,693	—	6,634,693	5,344,841	1,733,203	7,078,044	443,351	
Oxford	8,810	9,791,306	267,248	10,058,554	7,738,363	2,317,600	10,055,963	—	2,591
Penobscot	17,407	20,753,838	654,313	21,408,151	17,670,091	5,980,711	23,630,802	2,242,651	
Piscataquis	3,622	3,342,236	1,913,510	5,255,746	3,152,670	997,012	4,149,682	—	1,106,064
Sagadahoc	5,182	10,297,215	—	10,297,215	5,792,893	4,127,749	9,920,642	—	376,573
Somerset	8,698	10,649,895	1,478,983	12,128,878	8,780,531	3,507,992	12,288,523	159,615	
Waldo	8,563	9,577,834	—	9,577,834	6,825,126	2,295,892	9,121,018	—	456,816
Washington	9,758	9,145,108	576,684	9,721,792	6,948,387	3,450,984	10,399,371	679,579	
York	15,604	22,423,960	—	22,423,960	20,999,239	4,989,578	25,988,817	3,564,857	
Total	160,569	$228,030,656	$7,948,060	$235,978,716	$191,861,821	$67,048,903	$258,910,724	$25,413,328	$2,481,320

NOTE.—There are no statistics of the separate valuations of personal and real estate for 1890, that we have been able to find. The total valuation of personal property in 1890 is 25.1 per cent of the aggregate valuations of the State, if the value of wild lands is added as valued in 1890. But that is believed to be a very low valuation. The valuation for 1890 is that of the Valuation Commission. That of 1890 is as returned by the town assessors. Wild lands are not included in the valuation of 1890. The net increase appears by this statement to have been $22,932,009. Adding wild lands at the same valuation as in 1880, the increase is $30,880,069. The report of the Valuation Commission may alter these figures, but it is hardly to be supposed that it will lessen them, and we think will show that the personal property returned by the assessors for taxation in 1890 will not exceed 24 per cent of the whole valuation of the State.

Table II—*The Following Table Shows the Debt (funded and unfunded) of each State, the Amount Raised by Taxation, for State Purposes, and the State Tax on One Hundred Dollars.   Taken from Spofford's American Almanac.*

State.	Date of statement.	Amt of state debt	Amt of state tax	State tax on $100.
Alabama...................	Oct. 1, 1888	$ 9,489,500	$ 1,468,727	.55
Arkansas	Oct. 1, 1888	4,861,115	425,000	.40
California	July 1, 1887	2,698,000	4,455,383	.56
Colorado	Dec. 1, 1888	-	586,318	.40
Connecticut	Jan. 1, 1888	3,740,600	437,157	.12
Delaware	Dec 22, 1887	465,000	117,458	-
Florida	Jan. 1, 1888	1,273,000	367,197	40
Georgia....................	Oct. 1, 1888	8,752,303	1,372,605	.35
Illinois	Oct. 1, 1888	-	3,004,951	.44
Indiana.............. ...	Nov. 1, 1888	6,470,608	1,270,000	12
Iowa.	July 1, 1886	245,435	2,593,095	.25
Kansas	July 1, 1888	1,161,776	1,210,931	.41
Kentucky	July 1, 1888	674,000	3,572,434	.47 1-2
Louisiana	Jan. 1, 1888	11.982.621	1,566,120	.60
Maine	Jan. 1, 1888	3,959,000	1,021,021	.27 1-2
Maryland	Oct. 1, 1887	10,960,530	910.949	.18 3-4
Massachusetts	Jan. 1, 1888	31,429.681	5,321,234	.11 1-2
Michigan	July 1, 1888	239,993	1,950,085	.15 4-10
Minnesota	Aug. 1, 1887	3,965,000	642,843	.15
Mississippi....	Jan. 1, 1888	2,935,258	831,124	.35
Missouri	Jan. 1, 1889	9,525,000	2,839,523	.40
Nebraska	Nov. 1, 1888	449,267	2,287,093	.75
Nevada	Jan. 5, 1888	380,000	236,305	.90
New Hampshire	June 1, 1887	2,966,363	400,000	.13 8-10
New Jersey	Nov. 1, 1887	1.396,300	2,743,754	.26 4-10
New York	Sept. 1, 1889	6,652,160	12,577,353	.35 52-100
North Carolina..............	Dec 1, 1888	14,540,145	515,674	.30
Ohio....	Nov. 15, 1888	3,416,465	4,943,574	.29
Oregon.	Jan. 1, 1889	.	315,000	.40
Pennsylvania	Dec. 1, 1888	14,852,589	6,495,704	.30
Rhode Island........	Jan 1. 1888	1,341,000	394,237	.12
South Carolina	Nov. 1, 1887	7,411,021	766,878	.52 1-2
Tennessee	Jan. 1, 1886	17,000,000	954,903	.30
Texas......................	Aug 31, 1887	4,237,730	2,027,518	.25
Vermont	Aug. 1, 1888	135,500	457,658	.12
Virginia	Oct 1, 1888	31,863,043	1,783,702	.40
West Virginia.....	Oct 1, 1888	-	766,205	.25
Wisconsin	Oct. 1, 1888	-	868,453	.15 1-10

Table III—*Savings Bank Statistics.*

Year.	Depositors.	Total deposits	Average deposits *	Invested in bank stock.	Real estate mortgages.	Number depositing over $500 each.	Per cent of average dividends	Reserve and special reserve.
1874	$ 96,799	$31,051,963	$320	$686,087	$7,853,259			
1875	101,326	32,083,314	316	893,589	8,666,484	-	5.9 +	
1876	90,621	27,888,764	306	998,749	8,156,544	15,950	5.2 +	
1877	88,661	26,898,432	303	1,018,049	7,496,441	15,892	4.1 +	
1878	77,978	23,173,112	297	976,044	6,231,695	13,464	4.2 +	$1,054,275
1879	75,444	23,052,663	278	993,937	5,383,617	5,950	4.3 +	1,451,099
1880	80,947	23,345,988	287	1,114,473	5,239,463	14,895	4.4	1,347,068
1881	87,977	28,361,401	301	1,199,463	4,984,511	27,118	4.3 +	1,542,087
1882	95,489	31,430,636	309	1,408,307	5,180,472	18,887	4.2 +	1,076,449
1883	101,822	33,516,729	308	1,535,108	5,216,629	20,840	4.2 +	1,180,279
1884	105,680	35,101,644	311	1,583,537	5,438,608	20,788	4.16	1,200,405
1885	109,398	37,364,394	321	1,708,111	5,645,969	22,827	4.05+	1,292,402
1886	114,691	39,475,138	344	1,900,238	6,113,414	23,743	4.09+	1,428,363
1887	119,229	41,283,614	346	2,120,065	6,352,794	23,826	4.	1,515,530
1888	124,562	43,786,168	357	2,303,575	6,407,247	25,269	4.14+	
1889	132,192	43,977,085	332	2,533,126	6,680,055	-	4.14	1,805,229

*The report of Bank Examiner Bolster for 1878, the last which gives data of the kind in an aggregate form, shows that there were in 1877 seventy-four depositors whose balances averaged over $8,000.

Table IV—*Showing Rate of Taxation and Amount of License and Agents' Fees of Insurance Companies in the Several States.*

State	ALL CLASSES		FIRE AND MARINE		LIFE		DOMESTIC		FOREIGN	
	Gross	Net	Gross	Net	Gross	Net	Gross	Net	Gross	Net
Alabama		1 per cent								
Arkansas		2½ "								
California									2 per cent	
Colorado		2 per cent.								
Connecticut	2⅜ per cent									
Dakota	2¼ "									
Delaware		1 per cent								
Florida										
Georgia										
Illinois		3 per cent.								
Indiana										
Iowa	2½ per cent.								2 per cent	
Kansas									2 per cent	
Kentucky	2¼ per cent								¾ per cent.	
Louisiana						2 per cent				2 per cent.
Maine		1½ per cent.								
Maryland			2 per cent.		2 per cent					
Massachusetts			2 per cent.		{ ⅓ per cent of tot'l value of policies in force. 2 per cent }	of tot'l value of policies in force.	2 per cent		2 per cent	
Michigan	2 per cent.		3 "						3 "	
Minnesota										
Mississippi	1 per cent									
Missouri										
Nebraska										
Nevada										
New Hampshire	1 per cent									
New Jersey										
New York							{ Fire, 2 per cent. }		{ Life, 2%; F.M ¼%. }	

North Carolina	2 per cent.	
Ohio	-	
Oregon	-	1 per cent.
Pennsylvania	Now 2 per cent.	
Rhode Island	2 per cent.	
South Carolina	-	
Tennessee	2½ per cent.	
Texas	-	
Vermont	-	
Virginia	1 per cent	
Washington	2 "	
West Virginia	2 "	
Wisconsin	2 "	

Table IV—Concluded.

State.	Annual State License.	Annual Fees for Filing statem'ts	Certificate to agents.	Net Receipts—How Computed.	Filing charter.	Local tax.	Reciprocal legislation.
Alabama	$100	$10	$2	Deduction—expenses, losses, ret. prem.	$15	—	—
Arkansas	—	10	1	Losses and commissions.	30	—	—
California	—	20			Prelim., $50	License fee in San Francisco	R. L
Colorado	—	50	2	Expenses and losses		—	—
Connecticut	$10	10	2	—	25	—	R. L
Dakota	—	10	2	—	10	—	—
Delaware	$200	10	2	—	—	Each agent to city, $50. Agents pay for each company. $10......	—
Florida	—	5	—	—	—		—
Georgia	Traveling agent of Life Co., $50.	20	3	—	20	Agent's license fee for each city in which he does business, $10.	R. L.
Illinois	—	10	2	—	—		R. L.
Indiana	—	5	2	Losses.	30	Fire & Marine taxed local rate on gross receipts	R. L.
Iowa	School fund, $50.	20	2	—	25		R. L
Kansas	—	50	2	—	55		R. L.
Kentucky	—	40	50	Return premiums and re-insurance.	40		—
Louisiana	—	—	—	—	—	New Orleans only requires it not exceeding ¾ per cent......	—
Maine	$20	—	1	Losses and returned premiums.	—	—	— —

		Examiner of Co., per day, $5		Losses (insured endowments not loss).			R. L.
Maryland......	$200	-	-	-	30	-	R. L.
Massachusetts..	-	20	-	-	-	-	R. L
Michigan	-	Examiner of Co., per day, $5	-	-	25	-	-
Minnesota.....		$20	1				-
Mississippi	F. & M. $1000, Life $750, Acc. $250	5	5	-	-	Each agent $15 to $40 Vicksburg, each Co. $125	
Missouri	-	50	-	-	50	Net premiums taxed like other personal property......	-
Nebraska......	-	20	2		50	Same as above......	-
Nevada.......	$100	-	-		-		-
New Hampshire	-	5	-		20		-
New Jersey ..	Life Co.'s pay for each agent, $20.	20	2	Losses and expenses.	30		R. L.
New York....	-	20	6		-		R. L.
North Carolina,	$50	-	-		-		R. L.
Ohio	-	20	2		23		R. L.
Oregon	-	5	-	Losses, re-insurance and expenses.	25	Gross receipts taxed at local rate	R. L.
Pennsylvania ..	Life $100, F. & M. $50.	20	2		25	-	R. L.
Rhode Island..	-	20	2		30		R. L.
South Carolina,	-	-	50		-		R. L.
Tennessee	F. & M. $200, Life $300.	60	6		10	Personal property and gross receipts subject to local rate ...	-
Texas.......	-	20	1		25		-
Vermont	$200	20	1		-	To county, $10	-
Virginia......	-	-	-		-		R. L.
Washington...	-	-	-		-		R. L.
West Virginia,	-	10	6	Losses, re-insurance and expenses.	-	Agt County Lic. $30.	R. L.
Wisconsin	-	25	2		25	-	R. L.

INDEX TO SUBJECTS.

REPORT.